The Gift of

Anxiety

Harnessing the EASE Method to Turn Stuck
Anxiety into Your Greatest Ally

Diante Fuchs M.A.

TCK PUBLISHING.COM

ISBN: **978-1-63161-195-7**

Visit Diante Fuchs' website
www.theunstuckinitiative.com

Published by TCK Publishing
www.TCKpublishing.com

Get discounts and special deals on our best selling books at
www.TCKpublishing.com/bookdeals

Check out additional discounts for bulk orders at
www.TCKpublishing.com/bulk-book-orders

Medical Disclaimer

Table of Contents

Introduction

Everyone is talking about anxiety these days. No small wonder why. You might be shocked to discover that back in 2017, the World Health Organization released global health estimates for "Depression and Other Common Mental Disorders" stating that 264 million people were living with anxiety disorders worldwide.[1] That was back in 2017. Things have escalated since then. A study published in the Lancet in 2021 estimated an additional 76.2 million cases of anxiety disorders have developed globally since the start of the COVID-19 pandemic.[2] In fact, depression and anxiety have been ranked in the top twenty-five leading causes of health problems worldwide.[3]

If you also struggle with anxiety, you are not alone, nor are you abnormal. The bad news is that these numbers appear to be rising and medical systems don't seem to be keeping up, let alone supporting wellness. How many people are stuck on waitlists to see counselors and psychologists for twelve months and counting? How many people have been dismissed by a doctor who says the problem is "just anxiety," then sent off with a pack of pills and the suggestion of counseling? Perhaps this has been your experience too. Something needs to change and people need help.

But failing medical systems are only a tiny part of the problem with our mental health. The waitlist you might find yourself on is not the cause of your anxiety. Sure, it may make things worse, but our problematic mental health systems are not the root cause of our issues. Anxiety is on the rise because of our perception of it.

Anxiety has received a bad rap. I would go so far as to say that anxiety is one of the most misunderstood emotions that we experience. And it is our misunderstanding of anxiety, combined with our general fear and intolerance of uncomfortable experiences, that drives our anxious states.

When you have been raised in a culture that does not know what to do with big feelings, anxiety can feel downright terrifying. Many people view big, messy feelings as a vulnerability and a weakness. Their view has likely been caused and reinforced by social norms and parenting styles when we use statements such as "dry your eyes," "man up," or "put your big girl panties on." Our parenting books have suggested ignoring tantrums and allowing children to "cry it out," which implies that feelings aren't valid and that if parents correctly "train" their children, then their children will "behave" better. What does this lead to? The belief that having big feelings and expressing them is "bad behavior" instead of just a normal, healthy part of being human. And the perception is passed on generation after generation. Is it any wonder why we have so much generational trauma when so many of us have been trained from a young age to suppress, ignore, or rage against our own emotions?

No wonder adults are so afraid of their own emotional worlds. When "negative" feelings, whether sadness, anger, fear, or anxiety, show up, we adults do everything in our power to push them back down again. It feels painful to feel our emotions sometimes, so it's better not to feel at all, right?

We worry what others might think of us when they see our emotions. We call ourselves "pathetic" and "weak" when we feel sad, anxious, or overwhelmed. And, worst of all, we begin to believe there is something wrong with us when we feel intense emotions. But feeling big, intense emotions deeply is just a normal part of the human experience.

Instead of learning to listen to our emotions and learn from them, we quickly try to get rid of them by reaching for the nearest pill, distracting ourselves with yet another task, or pulling away from those we love so they can't see us falling apart. We follow the unspoken rules for dealing with emotions passed down through the ages: Ignore them, suppress them, distract yourself.

Our emotions have become sorely misunderstood, perceived as enemies to be abolished instead of our inner guides that we rely on for survival. Our society has lost touch with the truth that anxiety is a normal emotional response. It is designed to protect us and serve our best interests. We have labelled anxiety a mental illness or a disorder and these labels have perpetuated our fear and intolerance of anxiety. It is time to re-evaluate our understanding of emotions and learn to embrace the gift of anxiety.

Is Emotion a Mental Illness?

In over a decade experience as a clinical psychologist, and more recently as an anxiety coach, I have come to realize that the mental health field is far from empowering. Mental illness, while more widely accepted today than it was when I was growing up, is still poorly understood and managed. I would even go further to say the term mental illness itself is problematic and contributes to a widespread misunderstanding of mental and emotional health.

I believe that some of the most common conditions we call mental illnesses could be much better understood as stuck emotions. Anyone who has not been able to fully feel their feelings or process their emotional experiences is likely to experience stuck emotions. All that time spent resisting and rejecting their feelings makes them feel damaged and unstable when their emotions inevitably come back up to the surface. The more unstable they believe they are, the more unwell they become, and the more stuck the emotion becomes, leading to a cascade of negative effects which we call anxiety, stress, depression, helplessness, and mental illness.

I suggest that we consider commonly diagnosed mental disorders to be a combination of stuck emotional responses and coping mechanisms. Depression, for example, could be considered stuck sadness. And in the same way, anxiety disorders could be seen as stuck anxiety. This is important because the way we perceive and understand these stuck conditions (or mental illnesses, if you prefer) directly influences how we seek to solve them. If you perceive your struggle as a stuck emotional response caused by habitual thoughts and patterns that are changeable, you will feel empowered and able to change. But if you believe you have an incurable mental illness or disorder that you can do nothing about, then you may continue to believe that there is something wrong with you and that there is nothing you can do to change.

A systematic review of 128 primary studies[4] showed that patients who were labeled with a mental illness by a therapist or psychologist saw themselves more negatively, felt socially isolated, and perceived themselves as unwell and less competent. The researchers shared that 72% of other studies that also explored the consequences of being labeled with a diagnosis reported people experiencing negative feelings such as resistance, shock, anxiety, abandonment, fear and anger. Being labeled with a mental diagnosis could leave you feeling ashamed, overwhelmed, and helpless because it's "out of your control." But the truth is, your anxiety can become a huge gift in your life if you learn to relate to it like a good friend instead of an enemy to get rid of. And that's why I'm writing this book because you deserve to know how to listen to, learn from, and let go of stuck emotions and old habits.

Anxiety disorder is the only disorder that directly names an emotional response itself as being disordered. For example, stuck sadness becomes depression, stuck grief becomes complicated bereavement, stuck coping skills become various personality disorders, and stuck anxiety? Well, we call stuck anxiety an anxiety disorder. The problem with this is that we are suggesting that the emotional response itself is an illness and something to be avoided. You don't want too much anxiety, right? You might be diagnosed with a disorder!

These narratives only strengthen our fear of anxiety and keep us fighting against ourselves. We struggle and strive to push our uncomfortable feelings away, which just makes them become stuck. With all this fear about anxiety, you may begin more desperate attempts to not feel anxious and then become more overwhelmed when the totally normal response of anxiety naturally shows up. As your overwhelm and desperation to get rid of anxiety grows, you may begin to feel more hopeless and stuck in the impossible task of suppressing and removing the totally normal and healthy emotional response we call anxiety. That's right, anxiety is a healthy emotional response that is designed to help us navigate our lives more effectively!

The Benefits of Anxiety

Feeling anxiety on a regular basis is critical to your health and wellbeing, but feeling stuck, overwhelmed, and completely hopeless is not. When you fail to connect with your healthy emotion of anxiety appropriately, it grows in intensity, becomes loud and intrusive, and leaves you with the inevitable feeling of overwhelm and hopelessness. Some might call this an anxiety disorder. I call it stuck anxiety. Whatever you decide to call it, it's not a disease, it's not permanent, and there's nothing wrong with you. You just have to learn to get your anxiety unstuck, and I will show you exactly how.

My reference to stuck emotions rather than disorders does not intend to minimize the gravity of emotional responses that have become so disruptive that they have ended up with labels such as post-traumatic stress disorder, clinical depression, or any of the anxiety disorders. It is not my intention to diminish the pain and discomfort that comes with experiencing anxiety so intense that it has kept you out of a job, wreaked havoc on your relationships and personal health, or made you unable to go out in public. Panic attacks and intense anxiety can be incredibly painful and disruptive. I regularly see the incredible pain and suffering caused by these emotional experiences with the clients I work with. I am merely suggesting that our understanding of the experience as "disordered" may be contributing to the sense of helplessness and powerlessness that many people feel when they receive a mental illness diagnosis. And many, many people are now getting diagnosed, more than ever before.

However, anxiety is a tricky "condition" to "treat." (And again, I put these in quotes because it is not a condition, nor should it be treated, as I will show you in this book.) But, in the beginning of my career, I tried everything I could to "treat" the anxiety my clients experienced. I bought all the textbooks, as any new psychologist does, and followed all the best evidenced-based practices that were suggested. I offered all the interventions you will invariably be offered by your therapist, if you have one, including relaxation training, cognitive behavioral therapy (CBT), and a range of breathwork, distraction techniques, and more. But I felt just as defeated (and baffled) when clients would return the following week with very little improvement in their anxiety. Many of them didn't even complete the homework exercises they were given. Eventually, I started screening referrals and would pass on those seeking help with anxiety to other mental health professionals because I knew that the advice I was giving to these clients was not helping them. I went through all those years of schooling and continuing education to become a clinical psychologist and I still had no idea how to make a significant difference in the lives of clients suffering from stuck anxiety.

What I didn't realize then was that I was missing an understanding of what makes anxiety move from being an ordinary emotional response to one that becomes debilitating. I still operated from the belief that anxiety was a problem and a disorder that needed "treatment." I could not fathom why all the interventions and strategies aimed at treating anxiety didn't always work. I knew there was so much more about anxiety that I had yet to learn and understand. I was trained in a psychodynamic-based therapy approach and I took additional training in ego state hypnotherapy, schema therapy, narrative therapy, and eye movement desensitization therapy (EMDR). I had become versed in acceptance and commitment therapy, mindfulness-based stress reduction, and additional cognitive behavioral therapy. And I called myself an integrative psychologist drawing on a myriad of therapy modalities to suit the unique needs of each of my clients.

But all that training still wasn't enough for me to truly make a difference in the lives of my clients who struggled with anxiety until I finally understood the difference between ordinary anxiety and stuck anxiety and how one transforms into the other. And at the core of this was an understanding that anxiety itself is never the problem. It is just a messenger. As with all messages, it needs to be heard and acknowledged. In short, we need emotional validation.

The experience of being validated and given permission to feel our feelings in all their complexity is a huge portion of mental health and healing. We all need to feel validated. Clients may come in feeling burned out (which means they are feeling a lot of anxiety and not sure how to handle it). They may have toxic relationships at work or at home that are causing anxiety. They might have faced serious health problems, financial problems, or midlife crises. But it is the space to truly feel and express themselves, alongside some useful therapy tools, that heals.

Your emotional world is a guide that serves a very important purpose. Your emotions, while sometimes painful, are not to be feared, dismissed, or suppressed. They are what make you the raw, messy, beautiful human being that you are. Being human means witnessing a kaleidoscope of experiences, from the ecstatic to the despairing, and everything in between. There is wisdom and beauty in all the pain and joy.

Don't let misguided societal norms and expectations blur the importance of your deep and complex emotional experiences. As we medicate and suppress ourselves into ever more "normal" states, we lose sight of what is truly normal: to feel and to know that when feelings become big and disruptive, they are a clear sign that things are not okay with us and we need to listen.

In fact, it is entirely possible to view your emotional world, and anxiety, as a friend, instead of the dreaded cause of emotional pain. Because, as you will see, our emotional responses, including anxiety, are there for very good reasons. They act as our guides through life if we let them. And as one of our guides, anxiety simply requires us to accept it as our friend and listen to it. The rewards from doing so can be a true gift.

From the outset, that may feel difficult, if not darn near impossible. I get it. At this moment in time, anxiety may feel painful, overwhelming, and downright scary for you. It may have even caused an enormous amount of disruption to your life. I have met with clients who have been disabled by anxiety to the point that they were no longer able to go out with their kids to enjoy an ice cream at the park. Some had to quit their jobs and were unable to travel, see friends, or even enjoy sex with their partner. They would say, and you might agree, that anxiety destroys lives. To suggest acceptance and seeing anxiety as a gift might feel like an insult. But know this: The path to getting unstuck lies within the anxiety itself. You do have what it takes to hear and validate your own emotions. You can get anxiety unstuck. And you don't have to struggle for months or years to turn things around once you understand how to validate your feelings and listen to them.

Of course, there is going to be some work involved on your part. Some of the work will require you to consider new perspec-

tives, feel big feelings, and let go of old beliefs an
have been keeping you locked in a struggle with yo.
iety. That is what this book and the four-step E.A.S.E. ..
is about. You will learn to gain a new understanding of yo.
emotional world, and anxiety in particular, that will allow you
to finally put it back where it belongs as the ordinary emotional
response it was meant to be.

How The Book is Organized

Chapters 1 through 6 focus on developing clarity around the experience of anxiety and how important it is to lean in and validate
it. Even though anxiety may feel like your enemy, it's your friend
and I will show you the process of befriending it. You will also
see how anxiety moves from an ordinary response to becoming
stuck. As I describe the problem of stuck anxiety, you might find
it uncomfortable to read. The descriptions may cut to the quick of
it and may be somewhat triggering. That's okay. They are meant
to be real and highlight exactly what is going on when anxiety
becomes stuck. And as you will see, a large reason why anxiety has
become stuck in the first place is our inability to look at it and feel
it. I encourage you to begin changing that narrative starting right
now. Know that you have already survived 100 percent of your
worst days. You have what it takes to hold space for yourself and
explore anxiety more fully. And besides, you cannot truly solve
a problem without knowing exactly what that problem is. This
means that we are going to dive right into the problem of stuck
anxiety so that we can be clear on the solution.

And there is a solution.

Chapters 7 through 11 focus on shifting your response toward anxiety so that you can put it back as an ordinary response
that does not interrupt you. This section offers a clear, easy-to-
follow solution to stuck anxiety and how you can get back to
living a life you love. It is here that I share the four steps (Em-

power, Accept, Shift, and Engage) of the E.A.S.E. Method with you—an approach that will help you begin regaining confidence, accepting anxiety, and shifting your focus back to the things that matter most in your life.

Chapters 13 through 15 take everything one step further in understanding the gift of anxiety and how you can use this powerful inner guidance system for self-development. Understanding the sometimes-hidden reasons for anxiety helps you identify areas of your life that may need attention. In this section, I will also share suggestions on how to truly listen to anxiety to create meaningful insights and change in your life, as well as examples of previous clients who have used anxiety as an ally rather than an enemy with remarkable results.

Each chapter includes a Time to Take Action section. These sections have been included to guide you in the process of changing your response to anxiety. They include thought-provoking questions to help you reflect on yourself, your beliefs, and the experience of anxiety. Where relevant, they also include action steps to begin responding to anxiety in a different way. If you enjoy journalling then I invite you to use the questions as journal prompts. Alternatively you can simply reflect on the ideas and concepts to increase your self-awareness or discuss them with a close friend, partner, therapist, or coach.

If you are anything like me, you may feel compelled to skip directly to the "how to" section and begin implementing the four steps of the E.A.S.E. Method. I urge you to stick with the order of the book because the beginning chapters offer valuable information that will allow you to implement E.A.S.E. more effectively. Also, at the end of every chapter there are some important action steps you can take to begin the journey of befriending your anxiety and getting it unstuck.

Remember, it is better to clearly understand the problem before launching into a solution. I'm sure you are eager to get your anxiety unstuck, so let's get started.

CHAPTER ONE
What We Resist Always Persists

I felt the tears begin as the disappointment of the day enveloped me. I had been trying hard to look happy and keep up the pretenses for my kids. I knew I needed to feel my emotions, so I went up to my bedroom, locked the door, grabbed a whole roll of toilet paper, and allowed every tear of disappointment and loneliness to descend. I was ready to tuck in and call it an afternoon, permitting myself some time to feel my sadness and sob.

It was my worst Christmas yet. We had relocated to the South Island of New Zealand just three months prior, which meant we didn't know anyone in our new town. All our closest family and friends were back in South Africa. Not to mention the fact that COVID-19 had completely ruined the potential for visitors to enter New Zealand. We were alone for Christmas—just us four. My husband, my two young kids, and me.

Now this may not seem like a big deal, but Christmas celebrations in our family traditionally included family members, celebrations, and festivities. Lunch involved at least three roast meats, a range of vegetable and salad dishes, and then a couple desserts to lock in the over-full, after-lunch nausea that is common to Christmas celebrations. All the excessive feasting was easier when we had a table brimming with guests and many hands to help cook. With just two adults and two kids (one of whom is a picky eater), this kind of spread feels wasteful, if not impossible to achieve. I started the day knowing things were never going to be the same. We decided to do Christmas our own way, choosing two favorite foods each to add to the Christmas feast and avoiding the big roast lunch altogether.

Sometimes changing things up helps distract you from what you're missing. Other times it becomes painfully clear that things are just not the same. And things were clearly not the same anymore. No matter how hard I tried to bring on the Christmas cheer, I continued to be aware of this gaping hole in my heart where family and roast hams belonged. And while I am aware that this situation pales in comparison to some of the pain and suffering you may have experienced with anxiety, it illustrates an important point about emotions. Emotions can be anticlimactic when you just lean in to them. My tears flowed for a few minutes and then started drying up. I had prepared myself to sob all afternoon and all I got was a few minutes. And then my thoughts naturally steered away from how awfully lonely I was and how sad I felt to the beautiful day outside and the possibility of going for a swim. Before I knew it, the tissues were in the bin, my face was less blotchy, and we had our bathing suits ready for the lake.

I could have soldiered on that day. You know what it's like when you push your feelings aside and just get on with things? I could have done that. Biting my lip, pretending to be fine, and putting on an insincere smile that everyone could see through. But I would have been irritable as I tried to keep it together, overly sensitive to comments made in jest, and snapping at my family in my desperate attempts to contain my sadness and not "let it ruin the day."

That's what we tell ourselves, isn't it? That we will ruin the day with our feelings if we let them out. And then we go ahead and ruin the day with our desperate attempts at containing those feelings, which only prolongs our suffering and makes it worse.

Most emotional responses will naturally subside after a surprisingly short time if we simply give them the chance to. Every feeling that we have ever had has come and gone. Even happy responses such as laughter naturally subside. They never carry on forever. Even when we wish they would. Our emotions naturally ebb and flow. Even the uncomfortable ones.

Taking myself to the bedroom that Christmas afternoon to cry was an act of self-compassion. I gave myself permission and space to feel. I didn't get mad at myself for feeling sad or worry about how I was going to ruin the day for everyone else. I just allowed my emotions to be there. I gave myself permission to cry. And, most importantly, I validated myself and my emotions. *Yes! I do feel sad and lonely. And I have every right to feel that way.*

I didn't argue with myself about feeling sad and I didn't get sad about being sad. I simply allowed the feeling to come and then pass naturally. It happens this way every time. When it comes to emotions, as with most things, what you resist persists.

We keep those feelings stuck and locked in place when we try to resist them and push them away. When we fight our feelings, we begin to have feelings about the feelings. We feel sad and then we feel sad about feeling sad. We feel frustrated that the sadness won't go away. Then we feel sad that we are "ruining" the day with the sadness. This is how we keep ourselves stuck in a pattern of generating an emotional response about an emotional response until we're so miserable that we make everyone else around us miserable too!

You've had this experience, right? When the tears begin to prick your eyes and you immediately feel embarrassed that you're about to cry. Your face flushes and you begin to feel intensely uncomfortable with the tears now brimming over the edge. You wipe at them quickly, apologize for how you're feeling, and then continue to feel more hot, flustered, and messy. The more you push the feeling away, the stronger it becomes.

How about when you felt anger? Feeling angry and then being told that you shouldn't feel angry does not make you calm down, does it? More than likely, it makes you angrier. And the more you think about being angry, the angrier you become.

Anxiety is the same. That initial anxious feeling pops up and most people begin to worry about their feelings of anxiety. *Oh no! I'm anxious again! What if I have a panic attack? What if I don't know what to say? What if this doesn't go away?* Every thought like this generates more anxiety, and soon you're feeling anxious about feeling anxious. The more you try to make the anxiety stop, the more anxious you feel about it not stopping. *Why won't the anxiety go away already?* All our resistance does is make the anxiety more intense.

Sadness, anger, joy, and anxiety are all natural human emotional responses. They are all designed to alert you when things are going well and when something is happening that is not in your best interest. These emotions are real and they carry an important message for us. They let you know when your needs are being met—or not. When you resist them, they persist because you're generating more feelings about the feelings. *I shouldn't be angry. Why do I feel so upset? I must be happy for the kids.* When you ignore or resist the feeling you remain completely unaware of your need that's not being met. When you're busy trying to push away your emotions, you push away the important message they have for you.

On the other hand, when you allow yourself to feel an emotion and validate the feeling, the emotional response can naturally subside because your brain and body understands: the message has been received. You have to learn to pay attention to your emotions, welcome them, and understand what it is that you need. The first step is validation.

Using Validation to Stop Resistance

Let's explore what it means to validate a feeling. Validation means to acknowledge and allow something. When you or someone else validates your feelings, you will feel seen, heard, understood, and acknowledged. You receive the message, "Yes, you are angry. And that's okay. It's okay to feel what you feel. There's nothing wrong with you." When you validate an emotional response, you acknowledge its presence and pay attention to the need that it is trying to get you to notice.

When you feel invalidated, it means that your feelings have been dismissed, rejected, or brushed aside (or that you perceive reality that way even if you just misunderstood the other person's reaction). You—or someone else—are implying that you don't have the right to feel this way or that you are intentionally overreacting or being silly. Invalidation is unhealthy and destructive because it creates shame. And when your feelings are consistently invalidated by yourself or others, you eventually learn to just suppress them (and therefore your needs) to avoid feelings of shame.

Now you might be wondering; what are the needs that emotional responses alert us to? Every one of us has core emotional needs. Jeffrey Young,[5] the founder of schema therapy, suggested that there are five core emotional needs:

1. To feel as if we belong and feel safe in our relationships.
2. To have independence and feel free to make our own decisions and take action in our lives.
3. To be able to freely express how we feel and share our emotions with other people.
4. To have moments of fun and laughter.
5. To have some limitations on our own behavior so we can create a sense of self-discipline.

Above all else, we all need to feel loved, accepted, and safe in our relationships. In fact, from the moment we are born we begin learning from our environment and caregivers what we need to do to be lovable and acceptable. People will go to extraordinary lengths to receive this sense of belonging and acceptance. Aside from this vital need, we also need to be able to make our own decisions and have some independence in our lives while feeling competent in our ability to function well in life. We need to be able to say how we feel and know that we will be heard and understood by the people in our life. We need to have opportunities for fun and laughter. And we also need to have healthy boundaries and limits to our behavior.

These emotional needs are present from the day we are born and continue to be as important for us as adults as they were when we were children. When we are growing up, we naturally seek to have our needs met. If the strategies we use to meet those needs don't work, we adapt to our environment and find other ways to get those needs met. That's why some adults yell when they want to feel heard and understood while others may whisper quietly. Some people may avoid speaking up at all because their emotions were invalidated so often that they began to believe that no one will listen to them no matter what they do. Children learn very quickly what they need to do to ensure their safety. They also discover what pleases those closest to them and how to win their love, acceptance, and validation. We all know instinctually that being accepted by our caregivers is critical to our survival, and we quickly learn how to adjust our behavior to try to win their approval and acceptance so we can survive.

Maybe you learned to finish your chores, do well at school, and follow the rules to please your parents and feel accepted. Perhaps you learned that staying out of sight, being quiet, and not asking for too much would keep you safe and win you a better chance of approval. Our experience in trying to get these needs met creates core beliefs about who we are and what the world is like. *If I don't feel like I'm being listened to, I must yell so they will pay attention to me and my needs.* These beliefs drive our behavior and teach us how to act in the world in a way that will optimize our survival and ability to get our needs met. They become the organizing principles for the way in which we function in this world, interact with others, and perceive ourselves. Jeffrey Young referred to them as schemas and they have a huge role to play in triggering anxiety, which we will discuss in more detail in Chapter 12.

Why We Need to Validate Emotions

Emotional responses are our guidance system to let us know when one of those core emotional needs is not being met and when our survival is being threatened. Feelings of joy, fulfillment, and satisfaction are usually experienced when our needs for fun and connection are being met. On the other hand, feelings of sadness might alert you to the fact that your needs for attachment and validation are not being met. Anger often arises when our needs are being blatantly ignored by others and we don't feel heard. And anxiety often arises when our need for safety is not being met.

If an emotional response pops up to alert you that your needs are not being met, pushing the alert away and trying to ignore it won't help you get that need met. In fact, by ignoring your emotional alert system, your brain and body must find a way to increase the alert so that it can be heard and accepted. Your emotional response will only get louder as that need remains unmet and your brain continues to yell for your attention. This is why resisting a feeling only causes it to persist (and often intensify).

Let's explore your experience of anger for a minute. People usually experience anger when a need has been ignored or brushed aside. For example, maybe your partner didn't tell you they were going to be late for dinner. You become angry that they are late because it feels as if they haven't prioritized you or considered you in their plans. If you share your anger with them and they tell you to calm down, you're likely to get angrier. Not only do you feel ignored by them in their planning, but your emotional need to be heard is also not being met. What would happen to your anger if, instead of being told to calm down, they said, "I see why you are angry. If that were me, I would be angry too?" I bet just reading that sentence made you calm down, right?

Not only is that an empathetic response to your anger, but it feels like your partner might understand why you feel annoyed. Validating your feeling means that your partner has heard you and is now prepared to consider what you're saying. This means you no longer have any need to feel angry because your need to feel heard and understood is now being met. As soon as we validate the need and the feeling, the emotional response can turn off the alert.

But you don't have to rely exclusively on other people to validate your emotions or understand you. I was able to validate my own feelings that Christmas afternoon. I was sad and lonely, and when I finally said to myself, "*Yes, this is sad and lonely, let's feel that,*" I was able to validate my sadness and the emotional response was no longer needed. I had seen and heard my own needs. You don't always need others to do that for you. All you have to do is pay attention when the alarm goes off, acknowledge your feelings, and figure out what you need (like a good cry).

How Resistance Makes Anxiety Grow Stronger

If ignoring, minimizing, or shutting out a feeling means it will get louder to alert you, then ignoring it long enough means it may become so strong that it limits your ability to do things you used to do easily like driving, going to work, or going out in public. When this happens, your emotions have become stuck. It can be painful and scary, but I don't consider it a mental illness. It's simply a natural consequence of relating to our emotions in a way that doesn't work long-term. Resisting our emotions keeps us stuck. Validating our emotions gets us unstuck.

Most mental "illnesses" we find in the DSM-5 are, in my opinion, stuck emotions.[6] The emotions were ignored, pushed away, and dismissed so many times and for so long that the person's emotional alert system is constantly on red alert. What we call "mental disorders" are really feelings that are loud and disruptive because they have not been heard or validated for too long. They are natural and healthy emotional responses to tough and painful situations. Your emotions are calling out to alert you that your needs are not being met. So many of us have been taught to blame our emotions or mental health when we are stuck, but it's the pattern of resisting and suppressing our emotions that makes us feel so overwhelmed, exhausted, and helpless.

Anxiety is a fundamental and ancient alarm system in your brain, and the sole function of anxiety is to get you to pay attention to threats (real or imagined) to keep you safe. The emotional response of anxiety, therefore, arises in response to the need for safety.

When you're asked to do a presentation and you think about the potential that your peers may laugh at you, as unlikely as that may be… Cue anxiety. When you are preparing for an important meeting with your employer and you're not sure if you're going to get that promotion… Cue anxiety. If you're moving to another city and you're afraid you won't like it there… Cue anxiety. When you're walking home alone at night and you're not sure if there will be a burglar in the shadows… Cue anxiety. And when there is a world pandemic on your doorstep and your health, your job, and your future is at risk… Cue anxiety.

Anxiety can feel very uncomfortable and those feelings can leave us thinking that anxiety itself is a "bad" thing. The alarm bells of anxiety, which include a racing heart, rapid breathing, pressure in the abdomen, and dizziness (to name just a few) can be intense. It's no wonder we try to do everything in our power to make anxiety go away. But because our responses to anxiety involve resisting it, ignoring it, and trying to push it away, we often make matters worse. We're so focused on turning off the alarm instead of putting out the fire.

As you're beginning to see now, emotional responses don't subside when we ignore them. They get louder and stronger. As anxiety rings the bells ever louder, with ever more uncomfortable symptoms, you may begin to feel desperate about the anxiety and afraid of the painful sensations.

At this point, you might find yourself in a doctor's office, worried about the physical symptoms you are experiencing or seeking medication to help stop the loud screaming of anxiety. More than likely, you will be handed the diagnosis of an "anxiety disorder," and medications might be suggested. As far as I'm concerned, you have a classic case of "stuck anxiety." You do not have a disorder or a mental illness. When we think anxiety is the enemy, we go to war with our own emotional alert system that is designed to protect us. And when that happens, all kinds of things can start to go wrong. The pain and symptoms caused by stuck anxiety can be excruciating and exhausting physically, mentally, and emotionally.

The first step to healing and reversing this vicious cycle is to practice emotional validation.

Time to Take Action

You can begin this process of emotional validation on your own right now. Consider a challenging situation you might be going through. Now imagine your friend or partner was going through this challenge instead. Ask yourself how you would support them through the experience. What would you say to them? The words you use to console and validate them now become the words you can use in your own self-talk. This is how you can begin to acknowledge and validate your own emotional responses. If you would like to take this a little deeper, use the questions below to aid in self-reflection. If you prefer to journal then use these questions as journal prompts:

- What is a familiar feeling that comes up for you? Is it sadness, anger, frustration, loneliness, or something else?
- Think about the most recent experience of this feeling. What was happening? Who were you with? What thoughts were you having?
- If your best friend or partner was feeling this way, what would you say to show them that you care?
- Think about a future scenario where you might feel this way. How might you respond to yourself in a way that is validating and compassionate?

Finally, take a moment to read your words of validation and see if you can feel a sense of validation, understanding, and compassion for yourself in your heart.

CHAPTER TWO

When Anxiety Is the Enemy

I woke up at 2 am to this strange, rasping sound coming from the edge of the bed. Startled by the noise, I sat up straight away.

"It's just me," my husband said. And then he continued to breathe strangely and erratically. It took me a minute to wake up myself and finally ask what was going on.

"I'm dying."

Wait! What?

This was my thirty-two-year-old, fit-as-a-fiddle husband, who rarely caught as much as a cold, telling me he was dying. We had no evidence for this. In fact, he hadn't complained of being unwell at all in the past six months. My brain just could not piece it all together. I was completely floored when later he went on to tell me that he thought he had a rare lung disease called silicosis.

Silicosis is a condition that miners sometimes suffer later in life after working 40 years in a mine. Or people who have worked with concrete all their lives. My husband was a plumber and had been working in plumbing for eight years. Some of his work was on new construction sites where concrete was being used, but he didn't have frequent exposure to concrete dust.

Yet he was convinced that the labored breathing and chest pain he had been struggling with for the past few weeks meant there was something horribly wrong with his lungs. His conclusion? An untreatable, fatal condition called silicosis.

On this particular evening, he woke up in the middle of the night to go to the bathroom and felt intense chest pain. He was breathing rapidly as he explained that thoughts of never seeing our two-year-old daughter grow up and get married were tearing him apart. He worried about what would happen to me if I became a single mother. The more he thought about these things the more painful his chest became until he was eventually rasping on the edge of the bed in utter distress.

"I can't breathe properly," he told me. "It's like this all the time and it's getting worse." And then he confessed that he had started smoking cigarettes on the sly after an extremely stressful run-in with a work colleague a few weeks ago, which he believed had made the situation in his lungs far worse.

"No, babe. You fell asleep long before me, and I was forced to listen to your snores earlier," I explained, more than a little baffled by the situation. There had been no rapid, labored breathing while he slept. That appeared to be the case only when he was awake. I thought back to the previous days and realized he had been extra nervous the last two weeks, worried about a particular work situation that hadn't gone according to plan. He hadn't spoken about it much, but it turns out it had been stressful enough to get him smoking again.

I turned on the light, wanting to get to the bottom of what was happening for him. As I saw his wild, scared eyes and rasping breath I knew in a split second that he was having a panic attack. It all made sense in that instant. The chest pain, the labored breathing, the racing thoughts of death and serious illness. And the fact that none of this was present during his sleep pointed to only one conclusion: anxiety.

As I shared my hypothesis of anxiety with him, the relief on his face was palpable. He trusted me and my clinical judgment as a psychologist. And while I couldn't fix all his emotional problems in that instant, I could easily recognize a panic attack when I saw one. Understanding what was happening in his body at that moment brought some immediate relief. He felt calm enough that we could discuss what had been going on. We sat on the edge of the bed while he explained what had happened two weeks before with a client at work.

My husband was four years into running his own plumbing company. Most of his work was plumbing out new builds in the upmarket estates in an affluent area. He had recently started working with a builder he did not know well and had a few plumbing projects in process with him. My husband is a perfectionist when it comes to his work. He prides himself on neat and tidy solutions and always checks and double checks his work. This is largely because the man struggles with some of the most serious impostor syndrome I have ever seen. He works hard at getting everything right because, deep down, he believes he is an inherent failure and that, at some point, he is going to be found out and identified as a fraud who shouldn't have been running his own company. In the world of psychology, we refer to this particular core belief as a "failure" schema.

How Core Beliefs Trigger Anxiety

Jeffrey Young identified maladaptive schemas as patterns of thoughts, memories, and feelings that we develop about ourselves during childhood and adolescence. Our early experiences with significant caregivers teach us what we need to do—or not do—to get our needs met and to be loved and accepted by our caregivers. Generally, we are not consciously aware of the schemas we learned during childhood but they are often retriggered by current events in which our needs are not being met. In other words, many of the patterns of relating to yourself, your emotions, and the people in your life come from your early childhood experiences. This isn't just a psychological cliche. It's literally how we learn to socialize and relate to others and ourselves as human beings. And it is very common for people to be totally unaware of these patterns, which is why working with a therapist can help you see your patterns if you're willing to listen to their feedback.

People with a failure schema believe they are incompetent and inadequate and will eventually fail at their undertakings. Consequently, they are generally afraid to try new things. So, they prefer to play it safe.

One of my schemas is "unrelenting standards," which means that I tend to push myself to do more or be better (an exhausting endeavor). I also tend to push those around me, like when I pushed my husband into running his own plumbing company in an affluent town and taking on projects that, deep down inside, he didn't believe he could complete. So, on that fateful day, he had a run-in with this builder, who had (unbeknownst to my husband) been tampering with the plumbing at the new build sites. The builder accused my husband of making a mistake with measurements when, in fact, the builder's own tampering had resulted in the misalignment of pipework. When the builder questioned the quality of my husband's work, that experience strongly activated his failure schema and plunged him into an anxious spiral of what if thoughts. *What if I get sued? What if I lose my company and cannot provide for my family? What if I lose everything and my wife leaves me?*

Every what if question just exacerbated the fear that he had failed and would lose everything, making his anxiety worse. But because he does not like to admit defeat to emotions (like many men), he hid his feelings and soldiered on. He kept going to that building site, kept meeting with new customers, and kept working. Each time, he kept pushing those thoughts that he was not good enough away, trying to ignore the mounting anxiety and shoving aside any uncomfortable feelings.

Going to War with The Symptoms

Eventually, his anxiety had firmly lodged itself inside his chest and throat, screaming as loudly as it could for him to pay attention. And still he chose to ignore it, smoke cigarettes to push it away, and find other means of distracting himself from the worsening feelings of anxiety.

By the time I found him on the edge of our bed, he had been struggling with anxiety for two weeks and was now experiencing a full-fledged panic attack. The possibility that his symptoms were, in fact, a result of anxiety provided some relief in the moment. However, it took him a while to fully accept this (as it does with so many who experience anxiety about their health). He chose to go down a long and arduous path of doctor visits and x-rays to rule out any physical conditions and he tried a range of medications. But let's be clear that each of those interventions, however, was an attempt to get rid of the anxiety and the numerous symptoms caused by his anxiety.

When the chest x-ray revealed normally functioning lungs, he was diagnosed with gastroesophageal reflux disease (GERD) and received a prescription for medication to treat this. The pain in his chest remained. His anxiety continued. He then struggled with nausea and was diagnosed with irritable bowel syndrome (IBS), with even more medication to treat that too.

With every doctor visit and new intervention, he continued to feel anxious about his health. Each time, he believed they had missed something and that the symptoms he experienced had a more sinister source. At the same time, I was ferreting through all my textbooks and clinical psychology lecture notes to figure out how we could treat the anxiety. I felt frustrated that I, a clinical psychologist, couldn't figure out how to help my husband with his anxiety. I was certain that he was not physically unwell because no test result or diagnosis had proven otherwise and all his symptoms were also symptoms of anxiety. I could not understand why he wouldn't (or couldn't) believe it too. But that is the nature of anxiety: when we are stuck in its grips, it can trick us into believing all kinds of bad things will happen.

His symptoms continued to worsen, and now included difficulty swallowing, persistent chest pain, nausea, and a sense that he was not in touch with reality. The more he focused on his symptoms and getting the "right diagnosis," the more anxious he became about what he was experiencing. And the more anxious he became about his experience, the more anxious he became that he would never be "normal" again. With that thought, he would create a whole new level of anxiety about losing his family. Thus, the vicious downward spiral of anxiety continued.

Getting Rid of Anxiety Is Not the Answer

At this stage in my career, I was still passing on referrals for those struggling with anxiety. I had come to a place in my practice where I simply did not feel useful or have the expertise to help the many clients who had landed on my couch desperate to get rid of their anxiety. I had tried everything I learned including cognitive behavioral therapy, relaxation training, breathwork, and distraction techniques with those clients without any significant progress. I felt inadequate and incompetent as a psychologist when the anxiety remained and the client still suffered daily. But here I was, faced with my husband and his worsening anxiety, and I couldn't just pass him on to someone else. I had to get to the bottom of it, so I whipped out those textbooks and kept doing more research.

I suggested breathing techniques, stretches, and getting out into nature. He researched specific guided meditations, visualizations, and even hypnosis audios online. I sent him for counseling to try cognitive behavioral therapy, which didn't help. He downloaded healing hertz sound bites to listen to and soothe his nervous system. We spent months researching different techniques and trying just about everything we could find. But nothing seemed to give the relief he was looking for.

Most people just want to be free from anxiety. They want to get rid of the tightness in their chest, the shallow breathing, the racing heartbeat, and the overall sense of dread. They will try every strategy under the sun to try to rid themselves of the painful experience of anxiety and all the sensations that come up when anxiety is present in their bodies. What we discovered was that all the researching and trying new doctors and new techniques to find relief was just an attempt to get rid of the anxiety. And all the attempts to push anxiety away actually just make it worse because the anxiety alarm system must find a way to increase its volume until we get the message. Our experience showed us why most people don't find relief from anxiety despite trying every intervention they can get their hands on. And we also felt, firsthand, how devastating it feels to try so hard and yet make no progress.

You see, wanting to get rid of the anxiety meant we were attempting the impossible. When you understand that anxiety is an ordinary emotional response, then it becomes crystal clear that you can never get rid of it, just as you can't get rid of sadness, anger, or joy. The desperate attempts to remove anxiety just end up creating even more anxiety. With every strategy we tried, we failed. Sure, the anxiety may have reduced, and in some cases, he even felt momentary relief. But then later the anxiety would return, as emotions always do. Because our goal was to get rid of the anxiety, he would constantly check in to see if he was feeling anxious. So, inevitably, we would both feel defeated and a little more anxious every time the anxiety came back.

Pretty soon, I started to become more anxious too. I wanted my husband back, and the more we fought the anxiety, the more anxious I became that things would never change. The more anxious I became, the more anxious he became that I would eventually leave him. And soon we were both heading down a path of spiraling anxiety, hoping, and praying the next thing we tried would finally be the "cure." In short, we just had so much anxiety. All. Over. The. Place. We were very stuck and we believed anxiety was the enemy that needed to be abolished. But no one wins when you fight anxiety. Instead, you must learn to work with it.

Thankfully, we eventually figured that out.

Time to Take Action

We all develop schemas or core beliefs based on our early experiences in life. It's time now for you to take a look and reflect on which schemas may be operating for you. Here is a list of the 18 Schemas as defined by Jeffrey Young. Look through the list and highlight or write down the top 5 that resonate with you most. See if you can think of any recent experiences that triggered these schemas for you.

Young's 18 Schemas

Admiration Seeking
People with an admiration seeking schema tend to seek the recognition and approval of others at the detriment of their own needs. People with this schema can become extremely hurt, angry, or reactive to criticism.

Unrelenting Standards
People with an unrelenting standards schema believe that whatever they do is simply not good enough and they need to strive harder. They tend to be hypercritical of themselves and others and may be described as perfectionistic, rigid, and extremely efficient at the expense of pleasure, relaxation, and social engagement.

Insufficient Self-Control
Insufficient self-control is a schema that points to an inability to tolerate frustration and, as a result, it feels difficult to control impulses and feelings. People with this schema feel that any dissatisfaction, disappointment, or discomfort is unbearable so they will try to do whatever they can to reduce those feelings even if their behaviors become self-destructive.

Pessimism
People with a pessimism schema tend to focus on the negative aspects of life and ignore, or play down, the positive ones. They tend to be hyper-vigilant, fearful, and anxious.

Self-Sacrifice
People with a self-sacrifice schema will tend to focus largely on voluntarily meeting the needs of others. There is a belief that if they focus on their own needs, they are being selfish and feelings of guilt may develop. They therefore give priority to the needs of others and sacrifice their own. However, over time resentment may develop toward others who do not notice and meet their needs. This is often referred to as people pleasing.

Social Isolation
People with a social isolation schema feel like they don't fit in anywhere or belong in the world. They feel misunderstood and isolated within their own family and social groups.

Emotional Inhibition
People with an emotional inhibition schema tend to withhold their own emotional expressions or impulses because they believe the expression of these feelings and needs might harm others, lead to retaliation, or lead to rejection. They attempt to protect themselves by trying to remain rational and keeping their emotions and feelings suppressed or minimized.

Mistrust and Abuse
People with a mistrust and abuse schema tend to mistrust others, fearing that they will intentionally abuse or misuse them in some way. They are often on edge and guarded around others and often find themselves thinking about how others might take advantage of them or hurt them in some way.

Subjugation

People with a subjugation schema tend to submit to the control of others in order to avoid negative consequences. They will ignore their own needs and desires in favor of the needs and desires of another person to avoid confrontation or conflict.

Abandonment

People with an abandonment schema have a belief that significant others will eventually leave them. They feel like the presence of others is unreliable and unpredictable.

Vulnerability to Harm

People with vulnerability to harm schema believe that imminent catastrophe will strike them and significant others and that they are unable to prevent this.

Emotional Deprivation

People with an emotional deprivation schema expect that others will never be able to adequately meet their emotional needs. As a result, they tend to feel isolated and lonely.

Entitlement

People with an entitlement schema believe they are superior to others or entitled to special rights. They hold the belief that they should be able to do what they want, regardless of what others think. The core theme here is often around power or being in control of situations.

Failure

People with a failure schema believe they are incapable of performing as well as their peers. They tend to feel stupid or untalented.

Incompetence and Dependence
People with an incompetence and dependence schema some-times feel helpless and incapable of functioning independently. They feel incapable of making day-to-day decisions and are often tense and anxious.

Enmeshment
People with an enmeshment schema tend toward an excessive closeness or involvement with one or more significant others (often parents) and, as a result, have struggled to find their own identity.

Defectiveness and Shame
People with a defectiveness and shame schema believe they are internally flawed and bad, that there is something inherently wrong with them, and, if others get close, they will realize this badness and withdraw from the relationship. The feeling of being worthless often leads to a strong sense of shame.

Self-Punitiveness
People with a self-punitiveness schema believe that people should be harshly punished for making mistakes. They tend to be aggressive, intolerant, impatient, and unforgiving, especially toward themselves.

If you prefer to journal, grab your pen and paper, settle into a quiet, undisturbed space, and use the following prompts to help you identify some of the core beliefs that may be present for you.

- Think about a challenging situation you face in life. What thoughts come to you when you find yourself in this situation? Consider what you say to yourself about yourself in that challenging situation. Then recall another situation and repeat this process. Notice if you see any behavior patterns or recurring thoughts that might hold you back or keep you stuck.

- What fears or insecurities do you have that you do not often share with others?
- What core beliefs do you have about how to win approval and acceptance? Are these core beliefs true? One way to figure this out is to ask yourself whether you would believe this to be true of other people in your life. For example, would you believe they should always do their very best or else they are not good enough? Or would you consider that they should always put other people's needs first or else they are being selfish?
- If you would not consider these beliefs to be true of others, why do you think they should be true for you?

CHAPTER THREE

When Anxiety Becomes a Friend

As our struggles with anxiety continued, I happened to be looking into mindfulness-based stress reduction as a therapy technique to use with clients. I attended a seminar and, while listening to the lecturer discuss attachment and the impermanence of all things, it slowly began to dawn on me that there might be a different approach to working with anxiety.

I perked up and paid a little more attention to what she was saying: that "everything changes, and nothing lasts forever," least of all our emotional experiences. The Law of Impermanence is the first dharma seal (or primary principle) in Buddhist philosophy and teaches that everything has a beginning, a middle, and an end from our thoughts and feelings to the cells in our bodies, the plants and animals around us, and the buildings we construct. Nothing is permanent, and everything is in a constant state of change. The Buddhists believe that any attachment to these impermanent physical or mental objects will cause suffering. No matter what spiritual or religious beliefs you hold, I am sure you can agree that nothing in this life really stays the same, no matter how badly we wish it would. And, as you will see, holding on to the desire to keep it all the same often causes so much of our pain and suffering.

When we hold on to an object and it breaks or gets lost, we are sad and grieve for that loss. In the same way, when we attach to a particular thought or feeling about how things should or shouldn't go, we can become frightened or overwhelmed. In other words, when we become attached to the idea that we should not be feeling anxiety and that we must get rid of it, then we become afraid when anxiety inevitably shows up.

Imagine, just for a second, that you knew without doubt that the emotional response you experienced would subside within a few minutes. If you truly believed that the feeling would pass, your experience of anxiety would not feel nearly as scary or overwhelming. You might just think to yourself, *sure, this pain in my chest doesn't feel good, but it will pass in a few minutes.* That sounds like a much more reassuring thought than *I might be suffering from a fatal lung disease or This anxiety is going to ruin my whole vacation!* If you knew the anxiety would disappear within a few minutes, you would feel confident, you wouldn't worry about it, and you would find that your anxiety would quickly subside.

That is what the Law of Impermanence suggests; that everything is temporary, and everything will pass. And it is what the lecturer was explaining when my ears perked up. That was the moment I realized everything we were doing to try to "cure" my husband's anxiety was actually making things worse!

Why were we stuck with nothing improving? Because we were firmly attached to the experience of anxiety. By continuing to believe that we needed to get rid of anxiety we kept it firmly lodged in place.

Holding On to Anxiety

Our incessant focus on getting rid of anxiety led to us thinking about anxiety multiple times a day. We would begin the day, from the very moment our eyes opened, assessing my husband's level of anxiety. And then we would do a run-down of all his symptoms. How was the chest pain? Was the breathing any better? What was his swallowing like today? With each focus on a specific symptom, we would draw attention to it, evaluate it, and then feel anxious that it was still there. Obviously, it was still there—we were creating it!

When you are attached to something, you hold it firmly in place. It cannot go anywhere with you gripping it so tightly. *But*

I am not holding onto it! I am trying desperately to get rid of it! I hear you. The thing is that every time you try to push it away, you are also anxiously checking in to see if the strategy worked. You might try a deep breath and notice some relief, then ten minutes later come in and check on your anxiety levels again. In this way you keep yourself firmly attached to it. Every time you focus on anxiety you bring it into awareness along with all your subconscious fears and beliefs about anxiety and set yourself up for disappointment when you inevitably feel anxiety again.

This is the paradox of all those strategies for getting rid of anxiety. On the one hand, we want nothing to do with anxiety. We don't want to accept it, feel it, or be with it at all. We try everything to make it go away. On the other hand, we don't want to let anxiety out of our sight. We check up on it frequently. We're always thinking about it. And when it shows up, we think there's something wrong with us. Many of us believe that if we stop looking at the anxiety, we might lose control of it and it will get out of hand and become unbearable. So, we do this thing where we push it away and then bring it in close (just to make sure it really is gone). Thus, we anxiously fixate on our anxiety, making it worse.

This is what my husband and I were doing with his anxiety. And suddenly, it made so much sense why all our interventions were not working. They were causing, in many instances, more anxiety about the anxiety. The key was to learn to accept our anxiety and allow it to naturally subside. That's what the Law of Impermanence suggests, right? Nothing is permanent, everything changes, especially our emotional states. So, we had to learn to just let the anxiety come without worrying about it. And understand that it is not there to harm us but to alert us to an unmet need.

Learning To Let Go

So, what was his anxiety asking him to pay attention to? What unmet need did my husband have? In the throes of his health anxiety, he would say the anxiety was asking him to pay attention to the symptoms of the more sinister illness he was facing. That is what stuck anxiety does, as you will see. It becomes anxious about itself. But before my husband became stuck, the very first instance of anxiety, what was that all about? What was the need it was alerting my husband to? And how could we listen if we were not prepared to sit with the anxiety and accept it?

We spent all that time pushing the anxiety away and throwing one strategy after another at it, but none of that allowed space for validation or listening. Thankfully, the mindfulness-based stress reduction seminar I attended gave us some guidance on what to do next. So, I raced home, feeling very excited about our new action plan. I informed my husband that he was to begin learning and practicing mindfulness. I believed it was simply a matter of learning how to be present in the moment without attaching to the thoughts and emotions that were passing by. If he could learn that art, then he would be able to sever his attachment to the anxiety and finally allow it to subside.

Easier said than done, as you can imagine.

Accepting Different Types of Anxiety

While some people struggle with social anxiety, and others with generalized anxiety, my husband struggled with a category of anxiety known as health anxiety. Health anxiety occurs when anxiety is fueled by persistent concerns that the person is physically unwell. Bodily symptoms are scrutinized and interpreted as signs that there is some underlying disease causing all these problems. People who suffer with health anxiety often feel afraid of the symptoms of anxiety, which then creates more anxiety and more of the physical symptoms they're worried about. For example, when their anxiety causes chest pain from tight muscles and shallow breathing, they imagine they might be suffering from a heart attack, and those thoughts cause more anxiety (and more chest pain). In my husband's case, he felt shortness of breath from his anxiety but he thought he could have silicosis and the fear of this created more anxiety and more shortness of breath.

Health anxiety is not "worse" than any other form of anxiety. The effect of generalized anxiety on your overall life, for example, can be just as frightening. Many people who suffer from generalized anxiety experience a foggy brain, lose the ability to concentrate and may feel like they lose their words. Eventually they lose all confidence in themselves and their ability to cope when they feel anxious. They become worried about being anxious because of what anxiety does to them. We can see a similar pattern with social anxiety. If you're socially anxious then you feel nervous about being around other people, especially people you don't know. You might worry that they will judge you negatively or laugh at you. You fear they will reject you. And the biggest concern you have is that they will see how anxious you are and that will be what sets you apart from the group. In all cases the anxiety feels like a really bad thing that will result in terrible consequences.

So regardless of the type of stuck anxiety you might be experiencing, if the symptoms or sensations of anxiety feel threatening, it will be very difficult to detach from it and allow it to pass. As a result, no amount of mindfully focusing on the breath or practicing mindful activities was helping my husband, who could not let go of the thought that something terrible was happening to his body, which caused more anxiety.

If you have tried mindfulness, meditation, or yoga with very little improvement, then you might find yourself nodding at this point. When the anxiety is screaming and you're feeling desperate to get rid of it, it becomes very difficult to remain present and detached from the anxiety. So, it was clear that something was still missing from the puzzle.

By this stage, we understood that accepting the anxiety and allowing it to be there was key to removing the attachment and fixation. But how do you go about accepting something that you persistently fear?

It made sense that we needed to remove the fear of anxiety itself.

Knowledge Is Power

Drawing on my expertise as a psychologist and my work with clients in private practice, I realized that feeling empowered is often an enormous piece of the therapeutic puzzle. When my clients could more fully understand what was happening to them and why, they began to feel more in control and less afraid. Giving clients the knowledge and understanding of how and why they are experiencing anxiety empowers them because they feel more confident and in control.

Perhaps you have been in the unfortunate position of meeting with a doctor who simply spent their limited fifteen minutes with you, diagnosed you with anxiety, and prescribed a pack of medication that would supposedly help. It's likely that the consultation did not give you enough time to get a full explanation of how and why that particular medication works, let alone how or why you became so anxious in the first place.

So, you are left to your own devices and quickly Google the name of the medication when you get home, only to find that you have been given antidepressants or even antipsychotics. That sounds pretty frightening, right? Not only are you dealing with the persistent stigma attached to mental illness and psychopharmaceuticals, but you were prescribed a medication that isn't even listed as a treatment option for anxiety!

My husband's first visit to the doctor ended up with the diagnosis of "anxiety" and a prescription for Prozac. He did what so many of my clients do and put that box of Prozac at the very back of the cupboard. He felt confused and afraid. The medication implied he was very sick and he still hadn't quite grasped how anxiety could be the cause of all the issues in his body. The doctor didn't have the time available to fully explain the diagnosis of anxiety or the treatment option being provided. Like so many people today, he left the doctor's office feeling disempowered and afraid.

Many people turn to Facebook support groups or social media to ask questions about others' experiences with anxiety symptoms and treatment options. Often they are met with such a wide variety of responses that it is difficult to sort out the useful from the nonsense, leaving them more confused and afraid. Information is only helpful if it helps you feel confident or more certain. Confusing or contradictory information can reinforce the cycle of overwhelm and anxiety.

So, you can see why psychoeducation (understanding the why and how behind a specific experience) is an important part of the therapeutic healing when you're handed a diagnosis or intervention. It empowers you with real knowledge and a sense of certainty that can help set your mind at ease when you have anxious thoughts pop up. I had to figure out how to empower my husband so he wasn't so afraid of his anxiety.

So we began to research as much as we could about anxiety and how it could cause the symptoms he was experiencing. And the more we learned, the less afraid he began to feel. It became easier to consider that the physical experiences were indeed from anxiety and not another serious condition. As you can imagine, understanding anxiety and feeling empowered made it far easier for my husband to begin accepting his anxiety. The more he was able to acknowledge and validate his anxiety, the more it began to naturally subside. He didn't need to anxiously check on the symptoms; he learned to simply observe them and let them go.

We stopped all the checking and began to shift our focus back to figuring out what set off the anxiety alarm in the first place. What was the need? Why did he become anxious? What was the message the anxiety was there to deliver?

A New Understanding of Anxiety

Leaning in and exploring the anxiety with curiosity, as I will show you how to do with the E.A.S.E. method, is how my husband discovered his fear of failure and the need for safety from this powerful schema. He understood that his brain desperately needed him to pay attention to what was going on at work that felt like a threat to his survival. He was afraid that he was failing at his company and was about to lose everything. This was his Failure schema in action, and it was the events at work that triggered his fears. Anxiety was just sounding the alarm, trying to keep him safe. As he gained a deeper understanding of where this anxiety was coming from, he felt more empowered. And the more empowered he felt, the easier it was to accept the anxiety, shift his focus, and get back to living life again.

It has been many years since that evening on the bed. My husband, who would describe himself as a somewhat anxious person, has not been derailed by anxiety again. Sure, he has experiences of anxiety (we all do because it is just an emotion), but he can simply be with, acknowledge, and accept the anxiety so that it naturally subsides. And it always does. Befriending his anxiety and learning to tell the difference between stuck anxiety and ordinary anxiety made a huge difference.

Since then, I have used our experiences and new understanding to empower many clients in one-on-one and online group coaching programs. I have helped countless people become friends with their anxiety by providing real information about what anxiety is, how it becomes stuck, and how it stays stuck.

I want you to know that the failure of all those strategies and interventions you have tried does not mean you are abnormal or damaged beyond repair. It simply means you have been attempting to get rid of anxiety. And as you can now see, any attempts to achieve this impossible feat only serve to create more anxiety in the long run. It's not your fault because you were probably following instructions from your doctor, therapist, or family. I want you to know that anxiety, as intense as it might feel right now, is not a lifelong condition, nor an illness. Your emotional response has become stuck and there is a clear solution to this problem: Understand your anxiety and learn how to befriend it and use it as the helpful response it was designed to be.

The following chapters will show you exactly how to go about doing that.

Time to Take Action

The first step in befriending anxiety is learning to let go. It's time to get clear on all the ways you hold on to anxiety with persistent checking. Grab a piece of paper or your journal and a pen and list all the ways and times you check on anxiety. Do you check on it first thing in the morning? What do you typically ask yourself at this time? Do you use a heart rate monitor or check blood pressure? How often do you check your vitals, if you do? Are there other ways that you hold on to anxiety and keep it in your sights?

Now that you have a clear idea of where you are holding on you can begin considering letting go. Can you take your smart watch off? Could you consider skipping the vitals check? Could you reframe your morning question to yourself and ask, "what can I be grateful for today?" rather than "how am I feeling?"

Befriending anxiety also means learning to see it as a useful, helpful, and appropriate response. Can you think of how and why it may have showed up the first time? This will become clearer in later chapters but you may use the following self-reflective questions to get you started.

- What was happening in your life around the time anxiety became more intense? Can you identify any stressful situations, life transitions, or challenges you were facing?
- How did you feel about yourself at the time anxiety became more intense? How did you see yourself? What beliefs did you hold about yourself and your life situation around this time?
- Is there anything about the situation or your feelings about yourself that felt familiar to you? Is there a time in your life previously where you experienced or felt something similar to this situation? What was it?
- What do you think the anxiety was asking you to pay attention to at the time of it becoming intense? Write down whatever comes to mind without filtering, analyzing, or judging it.

CHAPTER FOUR

Ordinary Anxiety vs. Stuck Anxiety

If anxiety is supposed to be a natural emotional response designed to keep you safe, why is it so debilitating? This is one of the biggest questions I get asked when working with clients who have anxiety. And it's an extremely reasonable question. So, before we launch into the how, let's just get clear on what it is that we are dealing with when experiencing stuck anxiety.

The confusion comes in because we don't seem to have another term for debilitating anxiety. Anxiety that has become problematic is still referred to as "anxiety." In contrast, sadness that has become debilitating is called "major depression," for example, and we seem to have a separate name for most mental health conditions that have caused impairment to our social and occupational lives. But anxiety that has become debilitating is still just referred to as anxiety. Our language doesn't do a good job of distinguishing between the normal emotion of anxiety and extreme anxiety, hence why I use the term stuck anxiety to differentiate it from ordinary anxiety.

I believe this language issue causes a great deal of confusion and gives anxiety a pretty bad rap. It means that most people are unwilling to accept anxiety as a real and valid emotional response in the same way they would accept their sadness, anger, grief, or joy. As a result, I have found it necessary to make a clear distinction between ordinary anxiety and stuck anxiety so that you can tell for yourself when you are experiencing the ordinary emotion of anxiety and when you are experiencing stuck anxiety.

Ordinary Anxiety Is a Useful Alarm

Imagine you have an important work meeting coming up. Your employer has requested to meet you at an unfamiliar location for lunch and plans to introduce you to some new colleagues. While you are not certain what the meeting agenda is, you do know it has something to do with your job description. It would be entirely acceptable to feel nervous for this meeting. And that nervousness would be anxiety.

That anxiety is a natural emotional response that sets off your internal alarm bells because there is something you need to pay attention to in order to ensure your survival. Your anxiety sounds the alarm because it senses that something might hang in the balance if this meeting does not go well. So, your anxiety alerts you to a bunch of different potential issues.

For example, your anxiety might be asking you whether you have a clean, ironed, and appropriate outfit for the meeting. You quickly dash to your wardrobe to ensure that the laundry has been sorted and you have something nice to wear. Breathing a sigh of relief, you continue with your evening. A little while later you have another flutter of anxiety. This time you wonder whether you know exactly where your employer wants to meet with you. Have you been there before? Will you know how to get there? Will there be parking in the area? Ideally, these worries make you spend some time working out the finer details of the situation, so that you feel more confident that you will get to the meeting on time and prepared. You are safe and nothing hangs in the balance. For now.

Until later when your anxiety knocks again, and you wonder whether you should have prepared something for the meeting. Did your employer's email request anything specific from you? Did you miss something in the agenda? Your anxiety wants you to pay attention because being unprepared could keep the meeting from going as well as you hope. So, you double check your emails to ensure you are well prepared.

With each action you take as a result of paying attention to your anxiety, the emotion naturally subsides. It doesn't need to be there anymore because you have taken steps to make yourself feel safe (by being prepared in this case). This is the course of ordinary anxiety. If it weren't for the anxiety, you might have slept in, driven to the wrong restaurant, and showed up in a dirty suit, potentially putting your financial wellbeing in jeopardy. You see, anxiety can be a gift when you understand it and work with it instead of against it.

In some instances, the experience of ordinary anxiety can feel very intense and powerful. Sometimes the anxiety is alerting you to something that feels a little more threatening. Putting yourself in a position where you believe you may be laughed at or ridiculed, for example, is a common cause for anxiety. This is because the primitive part of the brain recognizes that being accepted by a group is important for your survival. Food and shelter are easier to come by when you are part of a tribe, and the primitive part of your brain knows this. So, when there is a risk of being ostracized and cast out, anxiety will sound the alarm to alert you to this possible threat to your survival. This is especially true if you have already had unfortunate experiences of being teased, laughed at, or humiliated when you were growing up. If you then find yourself in adult situations where your acceptance is important (such as a networking meeting for example) then your anxiety might sky-rocket as it begs you to pay attention to the potential threat of rejection. Some people may even experience a panic attack as your body prepares to keep you safe from the perceived threat.

A racing heart ensures that you get enough blood and oxygen to your muscles. You may need this to run away quickly or fight for all you're worth. (Remember, we are talking about the primitive brain here, so it is all about fight, flight, fawn, or freeze to keep you safe). Rapid breathing also helps ensure more oxygen goes to your brain and muscles. The digestive system shuts down in order to focus all your body's energy on the systems that help you fight or flee.

You see, the anxious response is designed to get you on alert and ready to survive. The physiological response of anxiety in your body can be very intense, and it can feel disproportionate to have your heart start racing at a social event when you don't have a woolly mammoth or saber-toothed tiger to fight.

Rest assured; such a response is still within the realm of ordinary. And when you take the necessary steps to prepare, pay attention, and ensure your safety (in whichever way is possible and appropriate), the anxiety will subside because there is nothing left to alert you about.

Understanding The Internal Message of Anxiety

Dealing with anxiety, however, becomes a little trickier when you are dealing with internal threats, such as core beliefs being triggered by events around you. My husband's work situation had triggered the core belief that he was a failure, which left him feeling like everything he loved and cherished was threatened.

At the time, he was not aware of this Failure schema being triggered, and on the face of it, he couldn't understand why he would feel this anxious about a false accusation. No amount of rationalizing and telling himself it didn't really matter would make the anxiety subside. And that was largely because he hadn't consciously paid attention to the core belief causing the problem.

It is not always easy or even possible from the outset to see what the anxiety wants you to pay attention to. Very often, the cause of anxiety is the combination of an internal belief and an external event. This is where learning to listen to anxiety becomes especially important. The process of listening does get easier as you become more aware of your internal world.

Understanding Stuck Anxiety

As challenging as it may be to understand the message of ordinary anxiety, it becomes even more complicated when the anxiety becomes stuck. This is because the anxiety is now alerting you to itself. It has become stuck in a loop. But how does this happen? Very often, as is the case with every client who ends up in my programs, the initial alarm was not well tolerated or understood, and so it just kept on ringing.

When that happens, it means the rapid heart rate, palpitations, shallow breaths, dizziness, nausea, and other anxiety symptoms stick around even longer to make sure the alarm is recognized. The anxiety begins to interrupt your awareness (as it was intended to do), but it soon becomes the only thing you can focus on because it feels so uncomfortable. And the more uncomfortable it feels, the more anxiety provoking it can become when you try to get rid of the anxiety or resist it.

This is the point where ordinary anxiety begins to get stuck on itself. There are various ways in which anxiety gets stuck so let's discuss these in more detail.

The Four Trajectories of Stuck Anxiety

1. *Anxiety Becomes a Habit*

You might recognize this form of stuck anxiety in yourself if you are prone to overthinking and worrying. While you may not be conscious that you are experiencing anxiety about anxiety, the anxiety does not seem to subside.

Many people who have been diagnosed with the "generalized" type of anxiety disorder could fit into this category of stuck anxiety. Generalized anxiety is anxiety that has become pervasive (lasts a long time) and generalized (occurs in multiple areas of life). A person with generalized anxiety might worry about all sorts of things and feel anxious about several situations and events in their lives on any given day. They don't seem to have a clear trigger or reason for their anxiety, and it seems to be directed at a wide variety of situations with no clear cause.

If you are struggling with generalized anxiety you may feel as if you worry about everything, from what to wear in the morning to what you want to say at your book club meeting tonight. You may worry about whether you have cooked a healthy enough meal for your family and whether everyone will enjoy it. The anxiety, at varying levels of intensity, tends to stick around all day long and simply direct itself at whatever it is you are doing next. You may feel unable to get a break from feeling worried and nervous. While it may not disrupt your functioning so much that you are unable to go out or do things at all, it often comes with a persistent feeling of being on edge. This persistent sense of dread can be overwhelming and tends to suck the joy from many moments in life. Most people with this type of stuck anxiety are labeled worrywarts or pessimists, and they continually feel anxious about seemingly small and trivial issues.

How has this anxiety become stuck? It has become a habit.

We now understand that anxiety is an emotional response to get us to pay attention to a need for safety. This means that anxiety only pops up when something is happening (real or imagined) that convinces your brain that there is a threat to your survival. Your brain wants safety, and only once it feels safe can the anxiety subside. This makes sense from an evolutionary perspective. Imagine looking behind you and seeing a Sabertooth tiger stalking you. Now imagine your brain just decided to not feel anxious or scared. If that's how our ancestors' brains worked, none of them would have survived and we wouldn't be here today! Your brain is designed to stay on high alert until the threat is gone, which means your job is to identify and handle the threat so that you can feel calm and safe again.

However, these days we aren't faced with many Sabertooth tigers. Our challenges have also evolved and there are many situations in our lives feel unsafe because they feel out of our control. It may feel difficult to identify the threat or know how to get to safety. When a child loses a parent to illness or divorce, it can leave that child feeling insecure and abandoned. Anxiety is likely to rear its head here to signal that the child needs more connection to their caregivers, but there is nothing the child can do to make the parent return. Similarly, if someone sees multiple members of their family struggle with serious physical illness, it can leave them feeling unsafe and fixated on the ways that life is fragile. Anxiety will likely make an appearance then but there is very little most individuals can do to remove physical illness from the world.

There are so many examples of situations that can leave us feeling scared, uncertain, and unsafe that are beyond our means to change. Growing up with financial stress and watching your parents struggle, losing your job, a burglary, a natural disaster that destroys your home or belongings, canceled flight tickets, or dashed holiday dreams. Any one of the myriad ways in which life hands us lemons can create situations where anxiety would be well and truly justified. Unfortunately, none of those situations are within our means to change or control. Depending on a host of factors, some of us simply do not have the emotional resilience to cope well with these circumstances.

We all need some sense of certainty and stability to feel safe. The idea of something being beyond our control feels unacceptable, and we will do everything in our power to make our world as predictable, stable, and certain as possible. We make sure we are on time, organized, and prepared for any eventuality. This is the only way we can feel safe and curb the anxiety that comes with life's curveballs.

When we feel powerless to do anything about our circumstances, we may begin to worry. Worrying is something we can "do" about the situation. Unable to tolerate the uncertainty and chaos, we cannot simply sit by and let our plans unravel. We want to take control and do something about it even when the situation is completely out of our control.

One way people learn to cope with things that are out of their control is to worry. Because worrying feels like it is preparing for an outcome. At this point, the brain realizes that this is something we can do, and—just for the briefest moment—things feel a little safer. We can tolerate the uncertainty of it all because we are, at the very least, worrying about this thing we can't control.

This is how the brain forms habits. When we take an action that brings momentary relief or a slightly better outcome, the brain will recognize that and then store that behavior as an automatic action to take the next time a similar feeling of discomfort arises. This is called reward-based learning. And the brain does it with everything, which is how habits (even the unhealthy ones) are formed.

We've all experienced this in one way or another. A great example is the sugary treat you may habitually use to overcome your 2 pm mid-afternoon slump. It started the first time you reached for a chocolate when you felt tired. The sugar gives you a little dopamine hit and you feel good again. Your brain recognizes that a sugary treat will help you when you feel tired, which means you automatically crave chocolate the next time you feel an afternoon slump. That's reward-based learning. Your brain quickly learns what is needed for continued survival and then stores that action as an automatic pattern.

The problem is that your brain doesn't link the sudden drop in energy you experienced a little while later with the chocolate bar you ate two hours ago. The sugar helped short-term but made things worse long-term. This is how your brain and body become classically conditioned to repeat patterns of behavior that feel good in the short term but do not resolve the problem in the long-term.

Life, by its very nature, is uncertain and unpredictable. We strive to make things as stable as we can, but the reality is that future events are well beyond our control and there will always be something that we didn't manage to prepare for. As a result, there will always be situations that feel uncomfortable because they are uncertain. Going to a new hairdresser, starting a new job, moving to a new house, meeting new people, walking a new route. Almost everything we do in life comes with some level of uncertainty. And if we are unable to tolerate the emotion of anxiety we feel in response to that uncertainty, we may use worry to try to do something about it. We worry about where we will park, what we will wear, what we might say, and how we might come across to those new people. We worry about things in the hopes of making them more predictable and controllable.

Eventually, the habit is formed, and worrying becomes the go-to strategy for dealing with the unpredictability of life even though worrying contributes to anxiety in the long-term. When worrying has become a habit, anxiety gets worse, and then we get stuck anxiety.

2. *Anxiety Disrupts Functioning*

Another way that anxiety becomes stuck is when you become anxious about anxiety because it is a threat to your functioning. In most cases this begins with experiencing uncomfortable physical symptoms of anxiety. Many people feel so anxious about the symptoms that they go to a doctor to get a diagnosis, treatment, or reassurance. Things don't feel right in your body, and you want suggestions on how to deal with it. Your doctor might examine you, send you for some tests and conclude that it is "just anxiety." If you believe their conclusion, you will probably return home with the prescription medications and a referral for counseling.

You may notice that the interventions do not bring you the immediate relief from anxiety you hoped they would. Now, as the anxiety continues, you might find yourself really struggling to function properly. You might struggle with forgetfulness, feel edgy all the time, or experience restless sleep that leaves you tired and drained the next day. The more this continues, the more your functioning becomes disrupted, and the more you begin to worry about the experience of anxiety itself.

At this point, you may start asking the dreaded what if questions. What if I get anxious at work and need to go home? What if I don't sleep tonight and can't function tomorrow? What if I get anxious while I am at a party or event? What if my anxiety causes nausea and I can't find a toilet while I am out? What if I never get better?

What if questions are gasoline we pour on the fire of anxiety. They only generate more anxiety. And it is usually at this point that you feel anxious about being anxious. The alarm bells are ringing to get you to pay attention to the alarm bells. The louder they ring, the more worrying they become, causing more anxiety and louder ringing.

3. *The Symptoms of Anxiety Become a Threat*

Let's go back to the scenario of going to a doctor for the uncomfortable physical symptoms you have been experiencing. Now, instead of accepting the diagnosis of anxiety, your brain can't help but think the doctor must have missed something. It doesn't feel possible that the array of painful physical symptoms you're experiencing could be caused by "just anxiety." So, you begin to worry. And check. And keep checking to see whether the symptoms are subsiding or getting worse. *What's that pain in my chest? That wasn't there yesterday...* With each hint of another symptom, a new bout of anxiety is released, and more symptoms are inevitably caused. This is what happened with my husband.

You may also find yourself asking more what if questions. *What if this is serious? What if the tests missed something? What if I am never normal again?*

Each what if question generates more anxiety. And the alarm bells continue ringing about the alarm bells. You have now become fixated on your symptoms of anxiety. With each symptom, more anxiety is generated, which results in more anxiety symptoms to feel anxious about. This is another classic case of stuck anxiety, or what might otherwise be called health anxiety.

4. *Panic Attacks*

The fourth trajectory of stuck anxiety is a panic attack. What most people don't know about panic attacks are that they often happen in isolation. In other words, they do not occur at the time of an immediate threat. I find it is often people who have been suppressing and bottling up their stress and anxieties who then experience a bubbling over of this response at a later stage. It's a lot like leaving the lid on the pot to boil. The pressure mounts and eventually the pot is boiling over and releasing the pent-up pressure of steam. Most panic attacks happen when we are more relaxed, like watching TV, driving a car, or going to bed. This is when your defenses are down and anxiety has a chance to scream at you. That's part of why you might find yourself having a panic attack during what seemed like a relatively peaceful afternoon with no immediate dangers or threats to be found.

The thing about panic attacks is that the experience is so intense, with a racing heart and difficulty catching your breath, that they often feel like you may be dying.

This means that at the time of the panic attack, your brain believes you are facing certain demise. This is important. Why? Because when an experience is perceived as a threat to your survival then it is classed as traumatic. When someone has had a traumatic experience, they will likely have an acute stress response, which includes anxiety. Remember that anxiety is the alarm system designed to keep you safe by getting you to pay attention to potential threats. If you had a panic attack that your brain perceived as a threat to your life, then it makes sense that your brain is going to want to avoid having any more panic attacks. That is the acute stress response your brain and body have to the traumatic experience of panic. Any sign or symptom of a possible panic attack might cause your brain to sound the alarm to get you to pay attention. *"Was that a heart palpitation? Why am I feeling dizzy? Am I having another panic attack?"*

Of course, anxiety about whether you're about to have a panic attack does not exactly help you calm down and avoid a panic attack. Especially when your brain believes a panic attack is a threat to your life.

Very soon, the dreaded what ifs will begin. *What if I have a panic attack at the supermarket? What if I have a panic attack while I am driving? What if I have a panic attack and I am all alone?* Eventually you feel persistently anxious about having another panic attack and, as this goes on, turns into another classic case of stuck anxiety, or what might be diagnosed as panic disorder.

Shifting Stuck Anxiety

No matter the trajectory of stuck anxiety, it is possible to shift it. I use the word shift deliberately because we cannot cure you of anxiety nor can we get rid of anxiety. Remember that it is a natural emotional response. Hence it needs no curing and cannot be removed. But we can shift stuck anxiety back to the ordinary emotional response it was intended to be and allow it to subside naturally.

Doing so requires you to first recognize the patterns of stuck anxiety that you fall into and then take steps to undo those patterns. In the case of an anxiety habit, you still need to address the need for safety, which in this case is a need for certainty. Because it's just not realistic to attain a state of total certainty about anything in life, the goal shifts to being able to tolerate uncertainty. In other forms of stuck anxiety, it means that we need to remove the fear of anxiety itself. And that will require, just as with habitual stuck anxiety, that you are able to welcome and accept your uncomfortable feelings and then shift your focus.

Now that you understand the difference between ordinary anxiety and stuck anxiety, we need to have a look at the different phases of stuck anxiety, which will let us figure out the steps required to get it unstuck.

Time to Take Action

Deepening your understanding of your own anxiety and how it developed will help you befriend it. It is time to reflect on how your anxiety became stuck. Consider the four trajectories discussed above and reflect on the questions below. You might like to journal around the following prompts:

- Think back to the first experience you had of intense anxiety. What fears or worries did you have at the time? Where was your attention focused?
- What is your anxiety currently worried about most? Ask your anxiety to finish this statement: "What if…."
- What are you most afraid of happening when you feel anxious?

CHAPTER FIVE
The Four Phases of Stuck Anxiety

I quite enjoy dancing. A client once said that life was a bit like the cha-cha: two steps forward, one step back. While there is a lot of to and fro-ing, at least we're moving forward. At the start of my career, I felt like I wasn't making progress with clients who struggled with stuck anxiety. It was more like one step forward and two steps back. They did seem to make a little progress with interventions such as cognitive behavioral therapy and relaxation training, assuming they followed through with the homework tasks, but I noticed that the relief and progress was often short lived. They felt stuck in what seemed to be a self-perpetuating cycle, and so did I because, despite all my training, I still didn't know how to help them get unstuck.

Since gaining a true understanding of stuck anxiety through my husband's experience and developing the new perspective that I am sharing with you here, a very important piece of the puzzle has become apparent: not only does anxiety become stuck, but it also gets worse over time as the vicious cycle of anxiety feeds on itself.

It's as if the anxiety slowly grows, gaining momentum and strength. The anxiety about anxiety becomes the problem, and interventions that focus on reducing anxiety symptoms or simply managing the experience of anxiety do not address that problem. So, the cycle continues, and many of the interventions fall short, which contributes to the momentum of this vicious cycle.

Eventually, it became clear that in order to deal with this anxiety about anxiety, we needed a better understanding of this vicious cycle—or as many clients have called it, the anxiety loop. I identified four phases of stuck anxiety. My aim in doing so was to help you understand the different stages of stuck anxiety because when you know what the problem is you will have a far better chance of finding good solutions.

Phase One: Fear and Overwhelm

Most experiences of ordinary anxiety feel uncomfortable, but they always subside and seem to have a clear trigger or cause. However, sometimes the experience of anxiety can persist, and the symptoms of anxiety continue a little longer than usual. This is where the first phase of stuck anxiety begins, and it is marked by a feeling of overwhelm.

Any one of the four trajectories of stuck anxiety that we discussed before might belong here. The experience of anxiety, the symptoms, or panic may feel frightening or overwhelming and before long you're feeling afraid of your anxiety or your symptoms. This phase marks the start of true stuck anxiety.

Phase Two: Rejecting Anxiety

Most people feel desperate to get rid of anxiety and get back to being their old selves again. As a result, they try everything they can to make it go away. They might find themselves researching different breathing techniques, meditations, exercises, and programs. Many will decide to take prescription medications to make it stop. Others might enlist the support from counselors, coaches, and other mental health professionals. In some cases, these interventions will be enough to put an end to stuck anxiety. However, in most cases, they remain anxious about their anxiety.

This is because their perspective is that anxiety is bad, and so they must do whatever it takes to get rid of the anxious response. So they remain hypersensitive to even the slightest sign of anxiety and keep worrying that they might become anxious again in the future. And if they do experience anxiety (which they inevitably will because it is a natural emotional response), it catapults them back into stuck anxiety with worrying thoughts that they are relapsing or going backward.

The sheer force with which they try to push the anxiety away begins to render any strategies they try less effective. Here's why. Trying on a new yoga practice, for example, in the hopes of relieving anxiety should, according to the studies, be very effective. However, the practice of yoga requires mindfulness and a level of acceptance of the space in which you find yourself. When you are using this practice with a feeling of desperation toward the anxiety, then you might find yourself consistently worrying about whether the anxiety will subside. All that worry generates more anxiety and you may begin to feel frustrated that it is not going away. Your mind will not quiet down, and you cannot settle into the yoga poses with the mindful practice you hoped you would. The rejection of anxiety in the act of yoga has made the practice of yoga less effective. If your body is doing yoga and your mind is worrying, you will not get the same benefits as someone practicing with a calm mind and body. That's why one person can go to a yoga class and feel peaceful and blissful afterward and another person can walk out having a full-blown panic attack.

The same goes for trying meditation, mindfulness, and relaxation training. When you are feeling afraid of the anxiety and frantic to make it go away you'll always be looking over your shoulder to see if the strategy is working. If you're not relaxing into the moment, then you'll remain slightly anxious as you anticipate more anxiety. Then, when you realize that you are still feeling anxious, more anxiety is created as you worry whether anything will ever work to make anxiety go away.

In short, the more desperate you feel to get rid of the anxiety, the more anxiety you create in that moment by continuing to worry about when it will go away.

Phase Three: Hypervigilance

This is the phase where anxiety becomes most stuck, and it feeds off the second phase. Paradoxically, the more you want to get rid of anxiety, the more difficult it becomes to take your focus off it because you keep checking on the symptoms of anxiety in an attempt to keep it under control.

Just as my husband and I did with all our checking on his symptoms, you'll keep bringing the experience of anxiety and its symptoms back into your awareness, which keeps it firmly lodged there. Before long, anxiety is the only thing you can see because you're focusing on it more than anything else. There is no room to consider going out, making plans, traveling, or even intimately connecting with your partner. Anxiety gets in the way of everything. This phase really begins to take on a life of its own as each act of checking, not only generates more anxiety but also increases the compulsion to check on the anxiety, firmly locking you into the anxiety loop.

Phase Four: Avoidance

Avoidance is anxiety's best friend. I have yet to meet someone struggling with stuck anxiety who is not avoiding something important yet anxiety provoking in their lives.

What if questions are the gasoline to the fire of anxiety and avoidance is the match that sets it alight. In many cases, the what if questions make us feel so overwhelmed that we begin to avoid taking action and making progress. Avoidance can seem like the only viable way to cope with anxiety. In psychology, we call this avoidance coping. The aim of avoidance coping is to provide temporary relief from the anxiety by avoiding the thing the brain believes will cause more pain.

In the moment, you experience worry and anxiety about making an important phone call. So instead, you decide to put it off and avoid doing it. Immediately, you experience a slight relief from the anxiety, and your brain has learned what it can do to keep you safe… simply avoid things! Remember reward-based learning? This means that the next time you feel anxious, your brain immediately suggests you just avoid the thing you're anxious about. So, you cancel plans with your family or decide not to go to the supermarket today, and you experience immediate anxiety relief.

But the issue you avoided hasn't gone away. You still need to make that call. At some point, you will need to go to the supermarket and your friends and family won't take "no" for an answer forever. So, avoidance can't make anxiety go away nor can it address the issue that brought up your anxiety in the first place. Avoidance can only provide temporary relief!

The tricky thing is that each time you avoid you confirm to your brain that this task is, indeed, a very frightening and threatening thing. Because why would you avoid it if it weren't dangerous? You also confirm all those anxious worries, such as, *What if I can't cope?* or *What if I can't do it?* by saying *Nope, I can't cope* and *Nope, I can't do it.* And all that avoidance leaves you feeling even more overwhelmed and defeated.

As a result, the avoidance and defeat feed back into the first phase of fear and overwhelm, and the loop becomes self-perpetuating. The cycle will continue until you learn to shift your behavior and thinking.

Putting It All Together

As you can see, the four phases of stuck anxiety feed into one another.

What's interesting about these phases is that it is our response to the anxiety during each phase that decides whether anxiety grows stronger or subsides. You'll notice certain emotional responses arising toward the anxiety at each phase. For example, in the first phase, as the name suggests, you feel fear toward anxiety. This may evolve as you enter phase two and turn toward frustration, anger, and even hatred toward the anxiety. With phase three, you may begin to feel obsessed and fixated on the anxiety. In phase four, you begin to submit to the anxiety by avoiding situations because you feel helpless and defeated.

The way you respond to the anxiety is largely what pushes you from one phase into another. Feeling overwhelmed and afraid of your anxiety long enough can make you feel frustrated and start rejecting the anxiety. When nothing you try works, you become fixated and hypervigilant. And hypervigilance is exhausting, so once that state has gone on long enough, you end up feeling defeated and helpless. That helpless feeling in turn contributes to feeling overwhelmed and afraid again. The way you respond to anxiety is what keeps the anxiety looping through the cycle of fear and overwhelm, rejecting your anxiety, hypervigilance, and avoidance.

Think back to your experiences of ordinary anxiety before it became stuck. There was a time when you did not respond to anxiety with fear, hatred, or fixation. In those moments, you may have noticed anxiety, perhaps disliked feeling it, and then taken the necessary actions to ensure your safety—at which point the anxious response would have subsided. So, at that point, you didn't have a strong emotional reaction to the anxiety itself.

Things might feel very different now. Stuck anxiety comes with a lot of feelings about the anxiety you're experiencing. The fear, the hatred, the hypervigilance, and the helplessness. This means that you begin to feel a certain way about—and respond a certain way toward—your anxiety. In short, you form an unhealthy response toward your anxiety and yourself.

Dealing with stuck anxiety might leave you feeling like there's no way out, but that couldn't be further from the truth. You're right where you need to be right now as you begin to clearly understand this cycle and what contributes to it. It is helpful to know that your response to anxiety has been a knee-jerk reaction in attempts to keep yourself safe and stop the discomfort of anxiety. But now that we know what is going wrong, we have a better chance of setting things right.

If the way in which you respond to anxiety is the thing that helps feed the stuck phases of anxiety, then it makes sense that we need to change the way you respond to your anxiety to get you some relief. Changing your response to anxiety is the most effective solution to the problem, so that's what you'll learn to do in the next chapter.

Time to Take Action

Let's take a minute to reflect on how you might be feeling toward your anxiety and which phases it may be stuck in. You may find yourself cycling through all four of the stuck phases, but let's explore where you may be most stuck.

Consider all the thoughts and feelings you have toward anxiety. It might feel useful to write these down in a journal. Then use the summary below to identify which phase of stuck anxiety you might be in currently.

Fear / Overwhelm Phase

When you feel afraid of anxiety, overwhelmed by it, or worried about it.

Rejection Phase

When you hate anxiety, feel frustrated about anxiety, and just want to get rid of it.

Hypervigilance Phase

When you are obsessed with symptoms, worried about symptoms, afraid of symptoms, and always checking in on your anxiety levels.

Avoidance Phase

When you feel helpless and defeated by anxiety, feel embarrassed about being anxious, and feel ashamed of having anxiety.

CHAPTER SIX

Defining Your Response to Anxiety

The stuck phases of anxiety go hand in hand with how you respond to anxiety, which in turn affects whether anxiety gets louder or can naturally subside. Over the past decade, I have identified four specific response types that people have with anxiety. Three of the response types generate more anxiety, while the fourth allows anxiety to calm down. Ideally we would like our response to be one that gets anxiety unstuck. Let's explore each response type in a little more detail and see where you might place yourself.

Anxious Fixation

This is probably the most common response type with anxiety. It is certainly where my husband found himself. If you're responding to anxiety with Anxious Fixation you probably feel as if your anxiety has taken control and is running the show. You'll tend to feel increasingly overwhelmed by anxiety and afraid of what it is doing to you, so you become scared of anxiety. You'll find yourself worrying about the physiological effects of anxiety on your body, or you might worry about how anxiety is going to interrupt your functioning. And most of all, you'll be desperate to get rid of it. When you are not afraid of anxiety, you'll find yourself angry and frustrated by it. There is very little acceptance of the emotion itself, so it's important here to begin to accept and welcome anxiety and all its symptoms without overreacting emotionally. We'll discuss how to do this in more detail shortly.

People with this response type often find themselves in the Fear/Overwhelm and Hypervigilance phases of stuck anxiety. They cycle through trying to push their anxiety away by ignoring it or distracting themselves and then draw it back in by anxiously fixating on their symptoms or worries. This is how Sandra related to her anxiety.

Sandra was a single mother of two boys and had experienced a panic attack, which led her to seek support from me. She entered therapy having only ever experienced one panic attack. Sandra had become completely homebound, unable to go anywhere without the support of her mother, who had come from out of town to live with her after the panic attack to help care for the children.

Sandra would never have described herself as an anxious person before this and had managed as a single mother for two years with very little additional support. This meant that Sandra held down a full-time job and looked after her two young boys on her own. It also meant that she had lost any time for herself and self-care. She would tell you this was beside the point; I would beg to differ.

On the fateful day of the panic attack, Sandra was dropping her boys off at school. Her youngest was just six years old, so she liked to walk him to the gate of the school. As she gave her youngest a hug, she suddenly felt out of breath, with a cold, fearful shiver overwhelming her. She felt like she couldn't catch her breath and she thought she might faint. The sides of her vision became dark and tunnel-like, and she struggled to figure out how to get back to her car. Thankfully her son had skipped off to his classroom, but Sandra was left standing there gasping for breath, feeling dizzy, confused, and scared. Her left side felt numb and her brain foggy, and somewhere amid this confusion, she had a clear thought that she was having a stroke. This thought sparked a new wave of fear and she collapsed to the ground, where her friend saw her and helped her back to her car.

The ambulance was called, as was Sandra's mother, and she was taken to the hospital for assessment and treatment. Needless to say, Sandra was sent home before the end of the school day with a clean bill of health and a diagnosis of panic attack.

She had never experienced anything like this before, and it was frightening. Thankfully Sandra's mother was able to fly out to spend time with her, and a friend collected the boys from school that day. But Sandra was afraid it would happen again. She was desperate not to have a panic attack in front of her boys because she was their only stable parent and didn't want to scare them. It seemed like it had come out of nowhere, and she was frightened it could happen again at any moment. She became hypervigilant, always looking out for signs that she might be on the brink of another panic attack.

Her fear about her anxiety became so bad she was unable to go anywhere alone. Her worst fear was that she would have a panic attack while out with the boys and no one would be there to help her or her kids. To protect herself and her boys from experiencing that, she avoided going out. She started to avoid taking the kids to school, grocery shopping, and getting out of the house on the weekend for a simple ice cream at the nearby park.

By the time Sandra reached out to me, her life had become completely interrupted by her stuck anxiety, and she was spending all day, every day checking her heart rate and oxygen levels. She developed shallow breathing, which also caused dizziness when she stood up too fast. The dizziness would spark new fears of an impending panic attack and even more symptoms of anxiety like a racing heart, sending her into another anxiety loop of fear and overwhelm.

While Sandra never ended up having another full-blown panic attack, she was stuck in a perpetual state of anxiety and fear about having one. Her response toward anxiety had become one of Anxious Fixation, and she spent almost all day checking her symptoms and feeling anxious about them.

Thankfully, Sandra saw how this response to anxiety was keeping her stuck. Through our work together she changed her understanding of her anxiety and her symptoms, and she gained the confidence to listen to what anxiety was alerting her to. When her perspective and habits of responding to anxiety changed, she was able to put an end to her anxious fixation and get back to enjoying her life.

Nervous Control

While Anxious Fixation is more common among those who struggle with health anxiety and panic attacks, Nervous Control seems to be the response type more common to generalized anxiety. Often, this response type is found in those who would describe themselves as healthy and "doing everything right." If you resonate with this response type then you might be someone who has learned the importance of self-care and will exercise regularly, eat relatively healthy food, and prioritize good sleep. When anxiety popped up, you felt confused and baffled as to why it has become stuck despite doing all the "right things."

In most cases, this anxiety has popped up after a major transition or life adjustment and then simply not subsided. In response you might find yourself increasing healthy behaviors like meditation and exercise and researching different strategies and interventions for anxiety. Your life is generally well organized, and you are used to feeling on top of things, so when anxiety becomes overwhelming, you are unable to tolerate it and try find more ways of gaining back control. The less control you feel you have, the more nervous you become.

People who respond to anxiety with Nervous Control are caught in the Rejection Phase of stuck anxiety and often try new and additional strategies to increase their health and functioning so they can control and reduce their anxiety. The more you try things that don't work, the more nervous energy you pump into trying to find that perfect intervention that will finally "make everything right." You may begin to believe you are simply not doing enough and might try longer meditations, more advanced yoga sessions, healthier diet plans, and research more options to finally get rid of anxiety. As the name suggests, more nervous energy is created with each attempt to control anxiety. To illustrate this point, let me tell you about Tash.

Tash's anxiety became stuck after her father passed away, and she was unable to shake the edginess, insomnia, and persistent nervousness she felt throughout the day. Tash described herself as someone who really prioritized her health. She engaged in regular exercise and yoga, and she followed a healthy Paleo diet. She prided herself on being healthy and organized. When she experienced anxiety that didn't subside, she couldn't figure out what she had done wrong. Tash attended a few counseling sessions with a nearby counselor to figure out the root cause of the anxiety and then she found me online. I coached her for a few sessions as we identified her Nervous Control response toward anxiety.

During the first session, I asked Tash what she had tried thus far to shift her stuck anxiety. I felt exhausted listening to her list off all the strategies and ideas she had implemented to reduce her anxiety and improve her sleep.

She tried a meditation practice before bed, essential oils, lighting candles, and drinking a new tea she had found at the supermarket. She bought special headphones to use while sleeping in case she woke and needed to listen to a calming meditation. She would wake earlier to do longer yoga sessions and took walks later in the afternoon. She found a longer route to walk and then attempted running as well because she had read somewhere that cardio exercise would help calm her nerves. She had attended a Reiki energy healing session, a body stress release session, a kinesiology appointment, and was researching hypnosis as the next alternative. Tash was completely determined to get her anxiety under control.

What I noticed most about her was the nervousness with which she went about researching possible interventions and the sheer energy she was putting into finding time to try all these new strategies and keep up her usual self-care practices. She looked and felt like she was on a hamster wheel. And her sleep kept deteriorating. I wondered whether she could simply be still and allow her anxiety to unfold. Naturally she was appalled at the idea. She was in a Nervous Control response toward anxiety, and she didn't want to let go.

With additional coaching and support, I encouraged Tash to simply allow anxiety to be without trying to control it or reduce it in any way. She cautiously reduced all the effort she was putting into keeping anxiety at bay and as she released some of the control, the nervous energy around her attempts subsided. Feeling marginally calmer, Tash felt empowered to learn how to lean in to and simply be with anxiety and the more she embraced the empowered acceptance of anxiety, the calmer and more in control she felt.

Shameful Submission

While this response type is less common, I often see it with clients who have experienced significant life challenges, including trauma and abuse, bullying, feeling like they do not belong in their family or social peer groups, or struggling to thrive at school (academically or socially). Shameful Submission tends to occur when your inner critic is strong and your self-confidence is low.

People who respond to anxiety with Shameful Submission would describe their anxiety as an ongoing issue, and often experience depression alongside their anxiety. If this sounds like you then the anxiety may feel loud and intolerable at times. When this happens you may begin to feel ashamed of yourself for struggling with mental health difficulties. You may believe you are a burden to others and begin to isolate yourself from social activities. You may feel embarrassed about your mental health and prefer to withdraw rather than reach out for help.

The anxiety, coupled with a strong inner critic, tells you how incompetent you are and that you are unable to cope. Your inner voice may say things like "No one really wants me around anyway" and "They are annoyed with me being anxious all the time." So, you tend to avoid other people, including friends and family. People with a Shameful Submission response to anxiety most often find themselves in the Avoidance Phase of stuck anxiety. The more you submit to the harsh, punitive self-talk and anxiety, the more embarrassed, ashamed, and defeated you feel. You might avoid or resist opportunities to receive support, gain confidence, or disprove negative beliefs about yourself.

Natalie was a clear example of Shameful Submission in action. She was desperate for help with her stuck anxiety after struggling for nineteen years. She attended one of my free online workshops and she really resonated with the information. She was eager to participate in one of my online group programs, so she messaged me to let me know she really needed help. Her message was hesitant, stating, "I really need help with my anxiety. You can say I have been very stuck. I am not sure anyone can do anything because it has been nineteen years—do you think I can overcome this? It's a long story, but nothing really works out for me. It is always like this, and it feels like I am always trying to fit a square into a round hole."

I was struck by the sense of defeat in her message, as well as the desperate plea for help but belief that she was beyond help. The tone of her message was embarrassed and ashamed of her struggle. Natalie did decide to join the group program but was unable to participate fully and pulled out after just three weeks. She messaged me to say that she did not feel she could contribute anything to the coaching sessions and felt too different from the others in the group. Natalie was also struggling with financial difficulties at the time and felt she could not afford the program payments. It was clear that she had decided she was beyond help and that the program was a waste of her limited funds.

In a way, Natalie submitted to the inner critic voice saying that she was not good enough or worthy enough of the help she was receiving. She believed that she was "too damaged" and "too different" to participate and, thus, ended her experience in the program. Consequently, she withdrew from support, removed the opportunity to learn how to create a different outcome, and continued to feel defeated and ashamed by her anxiety.

People with a Shameful Submission response to anxiety often avoid opportunities for growth, learning, and change because of their powerful negative self-talk and lack of self-confidence. If you truly believe that nothing is going to work, then why bother trying in the first place? This is the kind of thought pattern that keeps people in Shameful Submission suffering in silence.

Empowered Acceptance

Empowered Acceptance is where you want to get to with anxiety. People who relate to anxiety with Empowered Acceptance understand anxiety, how it functions, and why it's necessary. With this response type you would generally feel confident in managing episodes of anxiety and know that it will pass when the need for safety has been fulfilled. You'd understand that anxiety, in and of itself, is not a harmful emotional response, so you can just accept it when it arises. Of course, anxiety sometimes feels uncomfortable, but people with an Empowered Acceptance response toward anxiety will allow themselves the space to feel anxious without judging themselves for it or desperately trying to push it away.

Do you recall a time when anxiety was not stuck for you? I bet that back then, you might not have noticed every time you felt anxious. You may have called it "nervous" or "worried," and you simply accepted the way you felt. It's likely you didn't worry about anxiety and what it could do to you. You probably felt like you were able to manage any bouts of nervousness that popped up. You may very well have reacted to your anxiety the same way you do to anger or sadness. Realizing it is unpleasant, you'd likely wish it to pass, but you wouldn't spend all day every day checking to see if you were still angry or sad. You would let it go and carry on focusing on whatever it was you were busy with.

When you experience Empowered Acceptance of anxiety (and all your emotions, for that matter) then you accept your feelings as real, valid, and sometimes messy. The messiness of those feelings does not frighten you because you realize they are simply there to alert you to a need that is not being met.

Sadness, for example, often alerts us to feeling unloved, unimportant, invalidated, or unseen. Anger is often the response we have when our needs are being violated and not being heard. Joy and excitement are feelings associated with our needs for fun and spontaneity being met, while you might feel content and satisfied when you feel independent and empowered.

Empowered acceptance is not about being a perfectly emotionally stable human being that has it all under control. Not only is being perfectly emotionally stable an impossible task but I'd suggest it is even undesirable. Why? Because humans are indeed raw and messy. Our feelings are big, and we have the capacity to love fiercely, nurture unconditionally, and laugh until we pee a little. Why would we want to tame our humanity? But along with those "positive" emotions, we also have the potential to rage dangerously, become uncontrollably afraid, and cry big, fat, blotchy-face-making tears. Our emotions are real and valid. We do not want to eradicate them or suppress them. And they only become destructive when we refuse to stop and listen to them.

Empowered Acceptance means feeling strong enough to know that messy does not mean damaged, and that there is nothing wrong with feeling big, intense feelings. Empowered Acceptance requires that you trust yourself and your experiences enough that you will validate whatever it is you feel or experience. Whether you feel a little anxious before a first date or are panicking because life generally feels very stressful, you know that there's nothing wrong with how you feel. It means you know how to talk to yourself kindly and with emotional validation so you can think, plan, and act clearly even when big emotions come up for you.

Sadly, so many of us have not been given the opportunity to learn this. The stigma around mental illness has created a narrative that expects us to be calm, stable, and well-behaved. When big feelings arise, most of us are not taught what to do with them, so we choose to ignore them, distract ourselves from them, or medicate them away—anxiety included.

Your relationship with your emotional world—and anxiety specifically—may not be a healthy one currently. And that is what keeps those feelings stuck. Learning to forge a healthier dynamic of Empowered Acceptance between yourself and your anxiety is the most effective way to put anxiety back where it belongs as an ordinary, human emotional response.

Time to Take Action

Now is the time to identify how you respond to anxiety. Feel free to reflect on the descriptions of each response type and see which one you resonate most with.

You also have access to the free Anxiety Response Type Quiz at www.theunstuckinitiative.com/giftofanxiety

CHAPTER SEVEN

E.A.S.E. Step One: Empower

> It's time to break the cycle.
> It's time to heal.
> It's time to grow.
> —Unknown

A few years ago, feeling burned out and fed up with the confines of one-on-one therapy, I needed a change. The previous decade of therapy practice had solidified my understanding that acceptance and validation were key to healing stuck emotional states. But I wanted to expand, create real change in a specific area, and move beyond the restricted confines of a stiff therapy office.

My search to understand anxiety had revealed a vicious cycle and the unhealthy response types that keep it stuck. And by this stage I had a better idea of what was needed to shift stuck anxiety to normal anxiety for my clients. With my husband's firsthand experience of stuck anxiety and my expertise as a psychologist, I felt we had the potential to make a real difference on a bigger scale.

I started out with a small blog and began writing about anxiety. I built my expertise as an anxiety coach and worked with more stuck anxiety sufferers. Before long, I was explaining the specific stuck phases of anxiety to those who would listen and was frequently surprised by how moved they felt by the information. Just the understanding of that framework gave them a sense of validation and understanding of their experience. It removed the sense that there was something wrong with them and empowered them when they could see their anxiety as a natural emotional response that had become stuck. This knowledge helped them gain certainty, and the certainty calmed their anxiety.

This was the beginning of the E.A.S.E. (Empower, Accept, Shift, Engage) Method that I created to be a direct antidote to each phase of the stuck cycle of anxiety and help move clients toward an Empowered Acceptance response. So if you feel like you're stuck in a vicious cycle, know that you are not alone and the E.A.S.E. Method is designed to help you get unstuck.

Remember the four phases of stuck anxiety:

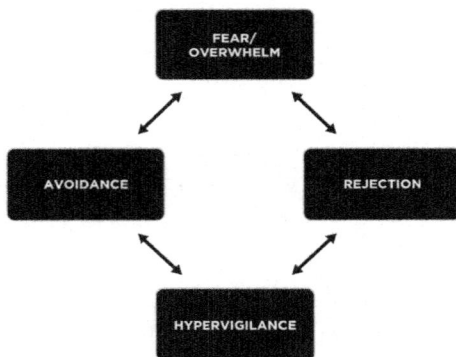

In the E.A.S.E. Method, you will now find:

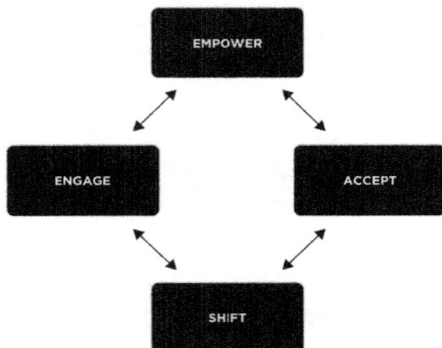

Step One: Empower

> The best antidote to fear is knowledge.
> —Robin Sharma

Maybe you find yourself in the first phase of stuck anxiety and, despite multiple visits to your doctor, you're still overwhelmed and afraid. This is likely because you have not received adequate information around anxiety, how it starts, why it stays, and what you could do about it.

The fear and overwhelm is not your fault. If it were that simple, you would have it all figured out by now. Those statements only serve to exacerbate the feelings of anxiety, defeat, and overwhelm because they imply that those with anxiety cause their own suffering. And as I am sure most stuck anxiety sufferers will agree, the cause of anxiety is far from clear. In fact, that is what makes it even more confusing and scary. With stuck anxiety, people do not seem to have control of the experience, and no matter what they do, nothing seems to help. Not the breathing. Not the medication. Nothing.

That is until they begin to truly understand their anxiety and learn from it. Because true understanding of anxiety would mean the fear is removed. To demonstrate, let me ask you this: Would you fear something that is designed to keep you safe?

Now, imagine you knew, without a doubt, that your symptoms were caused by anxiety, and understood that anxiety was there to keep you safe—would you still feel afraid of that tightness and pain in your chest? Most people would agree that, if they knew their symptoms really were caused by anxiety, they would feel less afraid of it.

However, I do understand that where you are right now, you may not trust anxiety even the slightest. And it is difficult to imagine it as a safe response, let alone a useful one. Once you begin to understand the mechanism of anxiety—how it functions in the brain and body—then the physical symptoms become more understandable. When you can answer the questions "Why me?" and "Why now?" then you will begin to understand your anxiety and that understanding will remove much of your fear and overwhelm.

This is why we begin with Empower, which is a two-step process. First, you must understand anxiety and how it functions. Second, you must understand why it has come up and become stuck for you in this moment.

Understand How Anxiety Functions

Let's start with the neuroscience of anxiety. Anxiety is a natural emotional response, and it originates in the limbic system of the brain. The limbic system is an ancient part of the brain that we share with all mammals, reptiles, and fish. So yes, dogs, turtles, and fish feel anxiety too because it's a natural hardwired emotional response that helps keep them and us safe and alive so we can pass on our genes to the next generation. The limbic system is also known as the emotional brain, and it's responsible for the basic functions of survival, including the fight or flight response.

Inside your limbic system, you have a watchdog called the amygdala that is always scanning the environment to check for threats and alert you to them. This watchdog can be more or less sensitive. In other words, you might find you have a big, stable guard dog that only barks for big perceived threats, or you might have a little chihuahua that yaps every time someone walks across the street. Think of your anxiety as the barking of your watchdog. It is the sounding of an alarm to alert you and get you to pay attention. The more "alert" your watchdog is, the more often it will sound the alarm.

Alongside your watchdog, you also have an investigator. This is the hippocampus, and it is the part of the brain responsible for assessing the situation and measuring it against available evidence to decide if it truly is a threat to your survival. When the investigator believes your survival hangs in the balance, it will trigger the release of adrenaline and kick off the fight or flight response. Let's explore how this works.

Fight or Flight in Action

Imagine you are sitting at your desk in your office and suddenly you hear the fire alarm sound in the building. Your initial surge of alarm is the watchdog (amygdala) giving a loud bark to get you to pay attention. You feel a wave of tingles flow through your body, your tummy tightens, and your brain goes into hyper speed. You are alert and ready for action.

At this point, your investigator (hippocampus) jumps into action and investigates the scene. You notice that others in the building are slowly making their way to the exit and a part of you remembers seeing an email last week about an upcoming fire drill. That thought instantly relieves your anxiety and you grab your office keys and make your way outside, feeling annoyed rather than afraid.

Now rewind a few moments, and let's imagine that your investigator looked out at the office to see people running around screaming about a fire. That wave of anxiety now increases with a surge of fear. Your heart rate increases, your breathing speeds up, and your guts feel like they're clenching. You have stopped thinking altogether now, and you run outside along with the others. You are now in a fight or flight response.

Adrenaline, the hormone released with your fight or flight response, is there to help you survive. It increases your heart rate to pump more blood to your muscles. Your breathing increases so you can get more oxygen to your muscles and brain. Your metabolism shuts down to preserve energy for the upcoming battle, and glucose is released into your bloodstream to provide more energy. All these responses in your body are designed to make you faster and stronger, either to run away or fight the threat head on.

This entire process is part of your anxiety response, and it will naturally create feelings of discomfort in your body. However, the symptoms of anxiety make sense when you understand how anxiety impacts your physiology. A racing heart can feel scary and intrusive but it's your body's natural response to a threat to move blood and oxygen to your muscles quickly. The pain in your chest makes sense when you consider how the small blood vessels of your heart need to contract faster than they usually do. That creates extra pressure in the area which you notice as pain, discomfort, or a tingling sensation. Your intercostal muscles (the tiny muscles around your rib cage) also contract, which can cause sensations of tightness in your chest. The rapid breathing (designed to get more oxygen to your brain and muscles) can make you feel dizzy as a new rush of blood and oxygen goes to your brain. The shakiness and jitteriness you feel makes perfect sense when you consider all that glucose, blood, and oxygen being pumped to your muscles to prepare your body to fight or run. As the Vagus nerve shuts down the digestive system in order to focus on the fight or flight response, you may experience reflux and burning sensations in your esophagus or chest. You may even feel nauseous, gassy, bloated, or other gastrointestinal sensations as your digestive system reacts to the rush of hormones like adrenaline.

Most people do not know how the symptoms of anxiety are created, which makes them feel afraid when it happens. But now you can understand why it feels so uncomfortable when lots of adrenaline is circulating in your system.

Sometimes you may find yourself having a strong anxiety response with no obvious threat around. The brain is hardwired for your survival so your watchdog will remember previous experiences that felt like a threat to your survival to protect you from similar events in the future. It keeps this information in mind when scanning your environment, and if something looks, smells, or feels like a previous threatening experience, it will begin barking once again. This can cause adrenaline to be released in situations that look completely harmless to other people. Now you're feeling anxious and afraid, and no one seems to understand why. You're not going crazy. That's just your brain alerting you to a potential threat based on your past experiences. You may not be consciously aware of what the threat is, but your brain and body are aware which is why you're experiencing the fight or flight response.

Here's an example: It's 8 am and time for your weekly office round up. You feel the blood drain from your face as your employer asks you to lead the morning meeting. You have attended this meeting for the past three years and know the routine that involves nothing more than a summary of the previous week and a discussion about new issues. It's boring, routine, and comfortably familiar.

But this morning it seems completely different because you have to lead the meeting. As you stand up to do what you have watched and participated in for three solid years, you feel like you might pass out. You completely forget what to say and stand stammering for just a second, with heat rising in your face, your hands beginning to shake ever so slightly. *What on earth am I anxious about?* you wonder to yourself as you stagger through the meeting.

Your watchdog saw you stand up in front of these colleagues and was taken straight back to a memory in fifth grade when Miss Lombard asked you to solve a math equation. It was a simple question, but you hadn't heard it because you were thinking about the peanut butter sandwich in your lunch bag calling your name. Standing up, you stuttered and gave the wrong answer, which had your friends and classmates in stitches of laughter. It was humiliating. And your watchdog recorded that memory so it could protect you in the future.

Your primitive brain knows that acceptance into the group is essential for survival. We find more food, better shelter, and more security in groups. A lone wolf is at risk. So, when we risk being ostracized from a group—be it through teasing, bullying, or being laughed at—the brain perceives it as a threat to our survival. In fifth grade, your brain recognized the threat and stored the information.

Now, a few decades later, the situation feels hauntingly similar. You're asked to stand up in front of your peers and say something…

Sound the alarm! The watchdog begins to bark. You'll be laughed at! Don't let that happen again! And now you're on alert, paying attention and feeling all sorts of anxious.

Later, you will tell your partner about the experience and wonder what on earth got you so anxious during the meeting. It will feel like a mystery.

Under ordinary circumstances, the evaluator will ascertain your safety and the alarm will subside. Sometimes, however, the hippocampus misinterprets the situation and sets off the fight or flight response in full. In most cases of stuck anxiety, your hippocampus has evaluated the symptoms of the alarm to be the threat. In this example, feeling dizzy and not being able to string your thoughts together may be the perceived threat that the hippocampus gets upset about. After all, a foggy brain has never been useful when leading morning meetings and could very easily result in an embarrassing situation. So, more adrenaline is released, which results in more dizziness and foggy thoughts. Now we have a self-perpetuating cycle of anxiety that seems to be increasing.

The more you understand about how anxiety functions and what happens during a fight or flight response, the more in control and assured you will feel when anxiety pops up for you.

Exploring Symptoms of Anxiety

You might already understand how anxiety works in the brain but cannot understand how this emotional response could be causing the specific symptoms that are worrying to you. Beyond the usual suspects of a sore chest, rapid heart rate, breathlessness, dizziness, and nausea there are a variety of anxiety symptoms that can feel scary and confusing.

I have worked with many people struggling with a blocked ear, for example, and their visits to the Ear Nose and Throat specialists have confirmed that there is nothing wrong with their hearing and there is no wax build up to cause the blocked feeling. They become worried and anxious about the feeling of fullness in their ear and struggle to accept that it could be anxiety causing this. The inner ear is extremely sensitive to changes in fluid and blood supply, which means that a racing heart and increased blood pressure can affect the nerves inside your ear. This sensation of fullness or ear pressure is common in people with anxiety and understandable when you learn how anxiety can cause the sensation.

You may be struggling with depersonalization and/or derealization (commonly referred to as DPDR) as a symptom of anxiety. Depersonalization happens when it feels as if your thoughts and feelings do not belong to you. They feel unreal. Derealization is the sense that nothing is real around you and you feel like you're living in a dream. One or both are, in fact, very common symptoms of anxiety although I prefer to see them as side effects of anxiety. You see, everyone experiences detachment or dissociation from their environment from time to time. We find ourselves on autopilot when we drive our cars or go through automated daily activities. It's that zoned out feeling you experience when you're driving or going through the motions of your daily chores. We also detach when things get stressful. When you get into an argument with your partner and say, "I don't care" and walk away, that's an example of detachment in action. Of course you care! You just need to detach from the stress for a moment so your body can calm down. When your emotions feel intense you may try to detach from those too and push them away to get a break.

Your brain may have learned that when anxiety gets intense and the situation feels stressful, the best way to recover is to detach from the anxiety. It is just a coping mechanism. But anxiety is something you feel internally. It is not an external stressor so the brain then tries to detach from this internal experience of anxiety. It's almost as if the brain is trying to detach from itself because anxiety often comes from our thoughts. This is what causes the feelings of depersonalization and derealization. Most of my clients share their fear of DPDR and believe it is a sign they are losing their minds. However, understanding that this symptom is really another mechanism to help you cope can reduce the fear and overwhelm you feel when it happens. Detachment is a normal mental response to a threatening situation when other responses don't work, just like anxiety is a normal emotional response to a threatening situation.

As you empower yourself with a better understanding of how anxiety functions you will feel more assured about the symptoms you are experiencing. Anxiety symptoms are vast and varied and it may be difficult to believe that the intense feeling of life not being real or the blocked feeling in your ear is just caused by anxiety. But you will be surprised to see just how many of the symptoms you experience and worry about are commonly experienced by millions of others when they feel anxious too. It is important to have a complete medical checkup to rule out any other causes but if your health-care provider gave you the all-clear then you should consider exploring how anxiety might be causing those particular symptoms.

As Robin Sharma once said, "The best antidote to fear is knowledge," which is why you need to Empower yourself with knowledge as the first step of the E.A.S.E. Method.

Understanding the Causes and Reasons

Now that you better understand your anxiety and how it affects your brain and body, you're ready to move toward a deeper understanding of why your anxiety has become triggered and stuck. Many people feel afraid when they can't figure out why they have become so stuck with anxiety. Removing the mystery and confusion helps to remove the fear and overwhelm. Clients often ask, "why me?" and perhaps you have too. When you answer the "why me?" and "why now?" questions for yourself you'll be able to foster more compassion for your anxiety. With compassion you can remove your fear of anxiety.

The first step of the E.A.S.E. Method will provide you with both causes and reasons for your anxiety. Causes and reasons sound similar but they refer to different aspects of what triggers (and explains) anxiety. I like to think of the causes as answering the "Why me?" question while reasons answer the "Why now?" question. Getting clear on both serves you in taking back the reins of control and putting anxiety back in place as an ordinary emotion. It feels far less overwhelming when you can understand why the anxiety is happening at this time.

Answering the "Why Me" Question: Causes for Anxiety

Understanding the cause of your anxiety means looking at the biological, environmental, and risk factors that are present in your specific situation and contributing to the development of stuck anxiety in your life.

For now, think of anxiety as a plant that grows. For any plant to grow, it needs a healthy seed. You can think of the seed as the biological factors, such as genetics, brain injury, hormones, etc., that increase your risk of developing stuck anxiety. It might help to ask your parents or caregivers if you experienced any birth trauma, head injuries, or significant childhood illnesses when growing up. Studies show that there is an association be-tween children who suffer meningitis and developing anxiety as adults,[7] for example. And there is enough research[8] to suggest that a family history of anxiety increases the likelihood of you struggling with anxiety yourself. The more biological factors you have present, the healthier your seed is and the more likely it is to grow into an anxiety plant. Understanding the biological contributing factors to your anxiety can also help you choose interventions that are more likely to be effective.

Just because you have a seed (healthy or not), does not mean the plant will grow. The seed will also need healthy soil. Think of environmental factors as being the soil. These include your early experiences growing up, your attachment with caregivers, your development through school, and any events that created the core beliefs you hold about yourself. Our early experiences are powerful, especially between the ages of 0 and 7 and again for a short period during adolescence. Our brains are developing during this time and soaking up everything in our environment to teach us how to do two important things: find love and accep-tance and avoid pain and suffering. We've already discussed how our experiences as children teach us how to get acceptance and safety in this world. Some of the core beliefs that were formed through these experiences may contribute to your anxiety.

Traumatic experiences are big contributing factors. You al-ready know that your brain stores all the experiences that did not feel good or seemed like a threat to your survival to keep you safe and help you avoid pain and suffering. So when a situation feels similar to a past traumatic experience, your brain quickly sounds the anxiety alarm to get you to pay attention.

You may not think of many of your painful experiences and memories as being traumatic. It helps to know that traumatic experiences can be separated into Big T and Little T traumas. Most people think of trauma as a big threat to life or integrity such as a motor vehicle accident, an assault, or extreme childhood abuse. These are our Big T traumas. You may not have experienced Big T trauma in your life but you probably have experienced other events that still felt traumatic to you at the time. Being laughed at by your peers when you couldn't answer the math question may be one of these Little T events. Or feeling scared and afraid when you were 5 years old when your mom was raced to the hospital without explanation of what was happening or when she would be back.

You may look at some of the Little T trauma events in your childhood as small and insignificant compared to other people's Big T events but the consequences psychologically and emotionally can be just as traumatic and painful depending on how you processed those events and emotions at the time. That's why someone can become debilitated with crippling anxiety after a seemingly "small" childhood event like getting laughed at in math class when you got the answer wrong.

Traumatic experiences are not the only environmental factors that affect how your anxiety functions. Any significant experiences during childhood could be possible contributors to anxiety. Children who struggle to perform at school due to learning difficulties like Attention Deficit/Hyperactivity Disorder (ADHD) or Dyslexia may experience lower self-esteem and develop core beliefs around failure and social isolation. Your world view and core beliefs about yourself are learned through the relationships you had with your parents, friends, and teachers as well as any impactful experiences you had as a child. You may have moved from town to town as your parents transferred from one job to another. You may have attended boarding school with a strict rules and regulations or become a high-performing athlete with extremely high expectations placed on you. There may have been sickness and adversity in your family. Or you may have observed a parent struggling with their own depression or anxiety. Each one of these experiences are likely to contribute to the beliefs you hold about yourself and the way the world works.

The more environmental factors you have present, the more fertile the soil is for the anxiety plant to grow in. In other words, the more likely it is for anxiety to become stuck at a later stage in life. A plant does not necessarily grow by just popping a seed into some soil. If you add water to the soil, though, you will usually have a flourishing plant. Water can be thought of as the risk factors involved. These include current stressors such as financial stress, work stress, environmental stress, toxic relationships, poor health and nutrition, substance use, and any other factors that play a role in triggering anxiety.

Perhaps you're struggling financially or live in an unsafe neighborhood. Your anxiety will be asking you to pay attention to anything that poses a threat to your survival. Working long hours with little time for family or self-care and relationships that are fraught with conflict and leave you feeling belittled and humiliated are also threats to your wellbeing. It doesn't matter how strong or tough you think you are, humans need self-care, rest, time to enjoy life, and healthy relationships in order to thrive.

Many people turn to substances such as alcohol, marijuana or painkillers to help them cope with challenges and uncomfortable feelings. While substances can provide relief from anxiety in those moments, there's no ingestible substance on this planet that can fix a toxic relationship or help you feel rested after working an 80-hour week. Any relief you may feel from the substance will be short-lived and the effect of the substance on the nervous system may create more anxiety in the long-term. Even the food you eat can affect your nervous system. Most of us know that caffeine can leave your nervous system feeling strung out, but so can sugar, many types of preservatives, and other inflammatory foods. This means that a poor diet is also a risk factor for anxiety. The more risk factors you have present, the more water is being poured on your anxiety plant to help it grow.

That is the garden of anxiety.

I have found that, once clients understand this garden, they have a better idea of where to focus their interventions and strategies. If, for example, you have many biological factors such as genetics and a recent brain injury but no significant traumas and a generally stable, happy childhood, then you know an intervention directed toward biology (such as medication, for example) will probably be better suited to your specific situation.

On the other hand, if you found few biological factors but many childhood experiences such as previous bullying and traumatic events in your upbringing, and an unstable relationship that's leaving you feeling disrespected and helpless then you may find therapy and lifestyle changes to be a better targeted intervention. Therapy may be aimed at understanding the dynamics in your relationships, exploring your specific interpersonal style, and uncovering the core beliefs that contribute to you engaging in difficult relationships. Lifestyle changes such as increasing exercise and nutrition, focusing on healthy coping strategies, and minimizing substance use may also be considered. These will be better suited to address the specific factors contributing to your anxiety.

There are a variety of different interventions and strategies that can be used and it is not a one size fits all approach. There are various medications, therapy techniques, and a multitude of healthy lifestyle options that can benefit you. Many people are overwhelmed by the various options and find themselves frantically trying as many interventions as possible. Your garden of anxiety will help you identify which of these are better suited to solve the problems underlying your anxiety. The point is, the more you understand about yourself and your anxiety, the more empowered and confident you will feel about accepting it and creating a plan that works for you. And accepting anxiety is imperative in stopping the loop of anxiety about anxiety.

Time to Take Action

It's time for you to do a little research on your own and figure out which symptoms you have that may be caused by anxiety. You can find a downloadable list of common and not-so-common anxiety symptoms on the resource page for this book: www.theunstuckinitiative.com/giftofanxiety

It's time for you to begin practicing how to get back in control over your anxiety when it pops up. So write down your anxiety plan of how you will respond when anxiety pops up. It could look something like this:

- Remind yourself of what anxiety is doing in your body. When panic sets in recognize that your body is doing an excellent job of keeping you safe and ready to run faster or fight harder. Write down the symptoms you experience and relate them to a function of the fight or flight response. This will help remove the fear of what you are experiencing and empower you in the situation.
- Use the anxiety symptom checklist on the resource page at www.theunstuckinitiative.com/giftofanxiety to normalize your anxiety symptoms. There are many symptoms that are associated with anxiety and knowing what they are will help remove the fear you may be feeling.
- Find out how anxiety causes a specific symptom you are worried about. There is always a reason for the symptom that makes sense.

Now consider the root cause of anxiety to help you feel more compassion toward anxiety and change your response toward it. If you're using a journal then I invite you to a grab a pen and work on understanding your anxiety garden:

- Write down a list of biological and physical causes for your anxiety.
- Now write down a list of the experiences you had as a

child that could be contributing to your anxiety and core beliefs.

- Lastly write a list of current situations or practices that could be risk factors.
- With this information you can decide where to target specific intervention strategies.

CHAPTER EIGHT

E.A.S.E. Step Two: Accept

The first step toward change is awareness. The second step is
acceptance. —Nathaniel Branden

When clients find themselves on my therapy couch or in
one of my online programs, they often complain that they have
tried everything and nothing worked to get rid of the anxiety.
When they refuse to accept anxiety as a natural response, they
find themselves relating to anxiety through Anxious Fixation,
Nervous Control, or Shameful Submission. It is powerfully
transformative when they begin to realize that trying to get rid
of anxiety is part of the problem.

We endeavor now to learn to accept anxiety. This is best
done in two stages: First, you accept the anxiety with no more
resistance. And second, you address the anxiety directly to validate it and calm it down by meeting your need for safety.

No More Resistance

It helps to begin viewing your anxiety differently. Instead of this
big, looming beast of a thing that threatens to destroy you, try to
imagine it as a small, scared child. Now imagine that this child
is so afraid because it wants you to stay alive. Visualize this small
child tugging at your sleeve, begging for your attention. They
are crying, afraid, and making a big fuss. The more you ignore
them, the louder they become. The more you yell at them to
stop, the more distressed they become. Few children will calm
down when an adult screams at them, becomes frustrated, and
says nasty things to them. It is far more effective to give them

a cuddle, demonstrate your understanding of why they feel the way they do, and then gently reassure them that everything is going to be okay. In doing so, you allow them into your space. To reassure them, you would have to listen to their fears, and that means accepting them. This is how it is with your anxiety.

When you have identified some of the causes and reasons for the anxiety showing up, you might find it extremely powerful to go directly to the source of the alarm to calm your amygdala. In the recent example of your morning meeting, you could consider reassuring the anxiety with some validating self-talk. *Oh, I see you there, anxiety. I know it was so painful to be laughed at in fifth grade, and I get why you would never want that to happen again. But we are older now and far more resourceful. Things are not the same, and I have sat through a morning meeting enough times to rehearse it in my sleep. Thank you for trying to keep me safe, but I've got this now.*

This is always going to require a very healthy dose of self-compassion. I have noticed that many of my clients are too quick to berate themselves for not coping or becoming too emotional. Calming your anxiety requires the ability to accept that you are fallible and that you, like all humans, do indeed experience big emotions. Sometimes we make mistakes and get it wrong. That is entirely okay. As an adult, you've got this. A lot of your current anxieties are rooted in earlier experiences where your survival depended on getting it right, being liked, accepted, and approved of. If you made a mistake at a younger age it may have felt unsafe and dangerous. Your parents may have been impatient with you or become angry with your mishaps. Perhaps you were met with disapproval or annoyance when you expressed your emotions. Getting it wrong may have cost you dearly.

Let's face it, if your caregivers had decided they didn't want you anymore, they could have simply cast you out. And your brain knows this. Your survival as a young person depends on being approved of by your caregivers. And remember that the primitive brain also knows that your chances for survival are strengthened when you are accepted into the tribe. So, the brain stores injured attachment relationships, and experiences of strong disapproval as Little T traumas and uses them to assess current situations in order to protect you. It then sets off anxiety alarms when current circumstances feel similarly threatening.

As an adult, your survival no longer depends on the approval of your caregivers. Yes, you are better off belonging to a group, and being ostracized is far from ideal, but you no longer need someone to provide food and shelter for you anymore. You are more than capable of surviving. Your internal resources, knowledge, and abilities have grown, and you have what it takes to take on challenges and weather disappointments. Your anxiety just needs to be reminded of this sometimes.

Talking to your anxiety can help you to foster some self-compassion and reassurance while calming down your alarm system. You might say something like, *Oh, hello, anxiety. I see you there raising the alarm bells and feeling worried. Thank you for trying to keep me safe. I am paying attention now.* You could continue by saying, *I've got the situation under control and am fully resourced as an adult to manage what is happening here.* Recognizing anxiety as the valid response it is and then taking over as the competent adult that you are will help to calm the anxious brain and quiet the alarm bells.

Leaning In

As we've discussed, sometimes the alarm bells are so loud and frightening that they result in more anxiety and alarm. While it feels counterintuitive, this is where truly leaning in will help the anxiety to subside. Leaning in is the process by which you are prepared to look at your anxiety with curiosity and invite it to be there with you. It means you are ready to explore the anxiety and all its symptoms.

Those two actions, exploring and being curious, will in turn create acceptance. The mere idea of exploring means you are interested in seeing more. Curiosity suggests an eagerness and interest in the subject. It seems impossible to be curious and willing to explore while at the same time feeling scared, defensive, or dismissive, right?

The aim, then, is to move toward the anxiety with curious exploration. I find it helps to simply breathe more. Literally. Most people feeling trapped with anxiety do not breathe fully. They are in a heightened state of tension, sometimes holding their breath or only breathing very rapidly with shallow breaths. The entire chest area is constricted and tense. These are natural physiological reactions to anxiety and stress. So, take a moment to notice your breathing and simply allow yourself to breathe more. Now, as you breathe, imagine creating more space inside your chest for the anxiety to exist within you. Stop all the resisting and contracting against the anxiety. Anxiety comes with a hunching of the shoulders, neck and shoulder tension, and a micro-contraction of the upper torso as you prepare to face the perceived threat. The entire physical state is tense, restricted, resistant—it is the body pushing back. With the breath, you open the chest and torso, and let go of the resistance. You literally create space for the anxiety to be there with you while letting go of muscle tension and the urge to push your anxiety away.

Now turn your mind toward the experience. Ask yourself what else you can feel with anxiety. Where does it manifest and what does that feel like? Perhaps it is light-headedness or maybe you experience a slight tingling in your hands. Become aware of the space anxiety occupies within your body. Notice the sensation and, as you explore your anxiety, remember to just accept your feelings without trying to change anything. You can tell yourself; *Anxiety is just an emotional response. It cannot harm me. I am feeling uncomfortable but I am safe and everything is going to be okay.* Stay with this feeling and state of mind and then take note of how things evolve and change. Because they always do. Simply observe, explore, and remain curious.

My clients really benefit from mindfulness-based strategies in their move toward acceptance. You might find these to be helpful for you too. Meditation is a mindfulness-based practice, but you don't need to meditate to achieve acceptance. There are a host of strategies you might try, but the essence of mindfulness is to remain present in the current experience without judgment. Simply observe and remain curious. There is no judgment of the experience as good or bad, too much or too little. It simply is what it is and you do not have to make it mean something. Feeling anxious doesn't mean you're going crazy or that something is wrong with you. Let go of those stories and judgments and just observe what is right now in this moment. When you apply this attitude toward the curious exploration of your anxiety, you will be practicing mindfulness at its finest. With time and practice, you will notice anxiety is just an emotion you experience from time to time. You will stop your mind from spiraling down what if rabbit holes and catastrophic scenarios. In allowing anxiety to just be there you end the cycle of anxiety about anxiety.

It may feel difficult at first but the more you work at this, the better you will get. Remember the purpose of acceptance is to allow anxiety in so that you can acknowledge it and validate it.

Imagine you had someone at your door. They believed they had information that would save your life and they desperately needed to tell you about it. They also knew you were home. Now imagine you tried to hide and pretend you weren't there. Or shouted at them to go away. Do you really think they would just leave? Remember, they believe they have life-or-death information to share with you and they desperately need you to hear it. Chances are, they will knock louder, shout through the door at you, and do anything to get your attention.

Anxiety is the same.

I know that anxiety can feel like a scary, volatile person out-side your door. It makes sense that you would not open the door to a person that behaved loudly and intrusively. But let's imagine you did open the door to this intense person to hear what they had to say. They might start out emphatically and frantically but they would then calm down as they shared the information they needed you to hear. As they began to feel that your safety was ensured, they would be able to calm down completely.

You do this with anxiety when you open the door, allow it in, and pay attention to it patiently and lovingly. The key is to meet the need for safety, which can only be accomplished once you have heard anxiety and acknowledged it.

As you explore with curiosity, you begin to listen to the anx-iety. You hear all the what if questions it is screaming at you. Perhaps you recognize how the current situation feels like a past one. And you understand the information the anxiety used is largely based on assumptions and information that is no longer accurate. Now is the time to placate and reassure your anxiety. We do not do this by pushing it away, ignoring it, or distracting ourselves from it. We reassure anxiety by addressing the infor-mation it shares with a touch of rational thought, some calming strategies, and a healthy dollop of self-compassion. This is the power of the second stage of Accept.

Meet the Need for Safety

Anxiety sufferers don't believe they can cope with the unwanted outcomes in their what if scenarios. This deep-seated and often subconscious belief that they cannot cope is what separates them from people who do not struggle with stuck anxiety. Experienc-ing anxiety may even be the unwanted outcome they believe they cannot cope with. While people who experience ordinary anxiety generally believe they can deal with whatever outcome they're faced with, stuck anxiety leaves you with a very different viewpoint. It abides by the belief that you simply will not cope with challenging situations. In a desperate attempt to keep you safe from these possible challenges, the anxiety begins to throw every conceivable problem and threat at you to help you prepare for the worst. This is how what if questions originate. Remember, what if questions are a powerful fuel to anxiety and they will keep you stuck feeling anxious unless you deal with them well. We've touched on these questions and their power to perpetuate anxiety, but let's understand them a little better because, once you come to recognize their wily ways, you will be able to put out any flames caused by these anxiety-producing questions.

My daughter calls them story snakes and realized at the tender age of eight that asking a what if question rarely makes you feel any better about a situation. In fact, what if questions simply take you down a worm hole of more what if questions and never provide a solution.

The trickery of these story snakes is such that the what if question is never answered. You simply ask what if and then feel the fear of the outcome without really understanding why. The story snake has you believing that it will be intolerable, and you will not cope if that outcome were to become a reality. When you don't answer the what if question, it just leaves you feeling even more anxious. The anxiety has you subconsciously believing you will die. Your survival is threatened by this potential outcome. But this is just a story snake and the pitfall of not answering the what if question. It is not true.

Let's use some examples to better illustrate this. Almost every client I have worked with who was struggling with stuck anxiety due to a panic attack has experienced the endless flow of what if questions surrounding the next potential panic attack. *What if I have a panic attack at the supermarket? What if I have a panic attack while driving? What if I have a panic attack outside the school gates?* Sound familiar?

You're asking these questions because deep down you believe you can't cope with another episode of anxiety. So instead of risking another scary situation, you decide to just stay home and avoid the situation altogether. Your mind is telling you that you can't cope with being anxious. No more grocery shopping, driving, or dropping the kids off at the school gate. Avoidance seems like a solution to anxiety, but it just makes it worse long-term.

People with generalized stuck anxiety often ask similar questions. *What if I am late? What if I forget what I was saying? What if I need a toilet while I am out?* Again, your mind is telling you that you can't cope with all the potential threats, so it gets you to focus on finding more ways to avoid all these imagined threats. You may engage in avoidance tactics like arriving a full half hour early, canceling events, or not going out at all. But any strategy you employ while still believing that you cannot cope with anxiety will not work for you.

You need to build a new belief that you *can* cope with anxiety and any imagined unwanted scenario and realize that your mind has been lying to you when it says you cannot cope. In fact, most people I work with have been coping with anxiety for a long time. They may not be functioning the way they would like to, but the fact is they're coping. When you look back at your life and everything you have been through, you will find quite a bit of evidence showing how you have survived, coped with, and even grown from past adversities. There is no reason to believe you don't have what it takes to cope with the what if scenarios your anxiety throws at you now.

Many people find that by simply acknowledging their anxiety and offering it reassurance and a sense of safety, it quickly subsides. Answering the what if question is a great way to meet the need for safety that your anxiety is screaming for. In these instances, simply continue with the questioning by asking, *Okay, so what? So, what if I am late? So what if I forget what I was saying? So what if I need the toilet?*

When you lean in with curious exploration and tolerate the anxiety that comes with the unwanted outcome, you begin to see a different option to the subconsciously perceived threat to survival. Perhaps having a panic attack at the supermarket is less than ideal, but as you answer the what if questions you realize you would simply find somewhere to sit and call your partner or close friend. Someone might come over and help you. It may be embarrassing, but by answering the questions, you can help your brain realize the situation is not as dangerous as it first appeared. You're essentially changing the belief from *I can't cope with this* to *It's not ideal, but I can deal with it.* Let me demonstrate how this works.

Story Snake 1:

So what if I have a panic attack while driving?
Then I'll have to stop and pull over.
Okay, so what if I must pull over?
Then I'll be panicking on the side of the road.
Sure. And then what will happen?
I'll call my partner to come meet me, or I guess nothing. I will just wait it out.

Story Snake 2:

Okay… So what if I'm anxious and need the toilet while out in public?
I guess I'll have to find a public toilet.
True, there are toilets everywhere. So what if that happens?
I might have to use a public gas station and it won't be a nice toilet.
Sure. And then what will happen?
Nothing I guess, it just won't be very nice.

As you see, you can do this with almost every what if question that arises and it will almost always end in the realization that you can, indeed, cope with the outcome.

Health Anxiety and The Fear of Death

It is true that some what if questions, particularly around health anxiety, will feel less comfortable to answer. These questions sound a lot like *What if I am having a heart attack? or What if the doctors missed something?* Facing the anxiety on the other end of these questions can be tough because they begin to touch on aspects around life and death, something most of us are not comfortable talking or even thinking about.

On the one hand we can answer those what if questions which will take you directly to your fear of death and the uncertainty around your mortality. It is a difficult conversation to have but the truth is, as Benjamin Franklin once said; "nothing is certain but death and taxes." And unfortunately, none of us know when our ticket will be punched. But if we think and talk about this more often, we can learn to remove the sense of overwhelming fear and anxiety many of us have when we think about death. Coming to a place of acceptance of our inevitable demise can help remove a lot of unnecessary anxiety.

We need to normalize death and dying. But our survival instinct is strong and we are hard-wired to do whatever it takes to protect ourselves from threats. This means that your brain will want to avoid death and dying as much as possible. And if it believes there is a threat to your life (like a potentially fatal illness, for example) then it is going to ring the anxiety alarm bells loud and clear. But the brain can get it wrong. Especially if you are already in an anxious fight or flight mode. It can misinterpret the signs and symptoms in your body and lead you to believe there is something threatening happening when in fact there is not. This is where we need to return to what we learned in the first step of E.A.S.E.

The Empower step has taught you about anxiety and its many potential symptoms. Your doctor has likely run tests that have ruled out the physical conditions your anxiety is alarmed about. Remind yourself of this and that you are, indeed, safe.

To address the need for safety you would need to address the anxiety as if it is a small child again. When little children express their seemingly irrational fears, we listen to them, validate their feelings, and try to reassure them. If they continue feeling irrationally afraid, then we may take a firmer stance, asserting our confidence that they are safe. We may say something along the lines of "Trust me, you are safe, and I wouldn't let anything happen to you." This firmer approach generally creates a sense of safety because someone who knows more has said it will all be fine.

I want you to treat your anxiety the same way. Once you have leaned in, listened, and acknowledged what it is asking you to pay attention to, you may need to take a slightly firmer approach. Because now it is time for you to take control and look at the facts. Take a moment to get present in the moment and turn away from your what if questions and swirling thoughts. Look around you and consider what is true in this moment. You might find the symptoms you experience right now do not meet the criteria for the health condition you are worried about. In fact, they very closely resemble anxiety. In this moment, you are ok. You may not feel fabulous with all those anxiety symptoms racing around but you are ok. Stay with that. It might even help to remember that your recent medical tests indicated you are safe and you can repeat in your mind or out loud, *I'm ok. I am safe.*

The only thing we can be certain about is what is happening in this moment, right now. We cannot foretell the future. Our memories of the past aren't always reliable. The what if questions are simply postulations and imaginings. We only have reliable, accurate access to what is present in this moment.

As you continue to stay with the present, answer the what ifs, and continue leaning in to what creates the anxiety, you might find yourself coming up with more rational solutions to the problem. This is how you can begin to create a sense of safety. You do not need certainty and you don't have to avoid life. You need to feel like you can cope with and tolerate whatever life brings your way.

Glennon Doyle once said, "You can do hard things." And I agree. The more you practice dealing with the difficult moments of life that create anxiety for you, the better you will get.

Blocking Beliefs

Despite your best intentions you may find it difficult to accept anxiety and just let it be. Most people fear that letting anxiety be means it will get out of control. But let me ask you this: When you have let yourself simply be happy and laugh freely, did that emotion become so intense and escalate out of control? No! It didn't and that is because all emotions naturally subside. But you may hold a belief that anxiety is dangerous somehow, and it's that belief that keeps you from accepting your anxiety and letting it be as you go about your life. It is your underlying beliefs about anxiety that drive your anxiety about anxiety. I call these beliefs blocking beliefs because they block your ability to accept anxiety. The reason this happens is that you (and your brain) will never accept something that is a threat to your survival. And if you perceive anxiety to be a threat to your survival then it doesn't make sense to accept it.

There are four main blocking beliefs that stop people from accepting their anxiety.

The first is a belief that anxiety or panic attacks can harm or kill you. Many people struggling with panic attacks worry that the intense anxiety they experience is damaging to their health in some way. They may fear heart attacks, strokes, or other complications they associate with intense anxiety. As a result, they find it extremely difficult to accept the anxiety or let the panic attack run its course so they continue to fight it and try to get rid of it in an attempt to protect themselves from their anxiety. If you still believe your anxiety is going to hurt you then you need to work on developing a better understanding of how anxiety and panic attacks affect your body. You can challenge this belief by learning about the symptoms of anxiety, how they make sense, and how they are designed to keep you safe. Once you understand that your anxiety cannot hurt you, you can let go of this blocking belief.

The second belief is that anxiety can make you lose control or go crazy. I have many clients who fear doing something irrational or dangerous when they become very anxious. They worry that their anxiety will escalate to the point where they will lose touch with reality and need to be restrained and transported to the nearest psychiatric hospital. Thankfully, anxiety cannot make you go crazy. Psychotic episodes and other psychotic disorders such as Schizophrenia usually develop in response to extreme trauma and stress. It is not possible for anxiety alone to cause these conditions.

While the feeling of anxiety or panic can make you feel like you are out of control, the reality is that you are still able to make decisions for yourself and behave in ways that are healthy and safe. You'll find that your panic attacks are barely noticeable to people around you. Despite how intense and chaotic it feels inside your head at the time, from the outside it probably looks like you're just fine. A client once argued that during her panic attack she had to lie down on the supermarket floor. Even her husband was embarrassed for her and wanted her to get up but she argued that she needed the coolness of the floor on her face. She interpreted this experience as one where she lost control. I disagreed because people that lose control of themselves don't normally have their wits about them to rationally explain their behavior. I have also met with people who have stopped their intense panic attack midway in order to help someone with a medical emergency. When you realize that you will always be in control of how you behave even if you feel overwhelmed and panicked, you'll be able to let go of this blocking belief.

The third blocking belief is that anxiety or panic attacks can disable you so that you can't talk, think, or function. Perhaps you worry that you will pass out from the anxiety or feel scared that you will not be able to communicate properly with those around you. I've had clients share fears that they will lose all ability to talk to their friends and colleagues if anxiety becomes intense. These common fears stop you from accepting anxiety because you think it will disrupt your ability to function. The truth is that fainting is usually caused by low blood pressure whereas anxiety creates an increase in blood pressure. It is almost impossible for anxiety to cause fainting. In rare cases, people may experience vasovagal syncope which causes the body to overreact to triggers such as the sight of blood or emotional distress. In these instances your heart rate slows and the blood vessels in your legs dilate, causing a drop in blood pressure, light-headedness, and possible fainting. If you're prone to vasovagal syncope then you have likely experienced this before with previous emotional distress or triggers such as when seeing a needle while getting a vaccine. It is unlikely to happen suddenly and come out of nowhere. This means that if you have not yet fainted during an anxiety attack then there is no reason to believe you ever will.

Finally, the belief that anxiety is shameful and embarrassing can be a serious block to accepting it and allowing it to run its course, especially in front of other people. If you struggle with the idea of letting others see you anxious, then you may hold this blocking belief about anxiety. Given how many people struggle with anxiety nowadays, you now know that you are not alone or abnormal. Sharing your vulnerability with someone else is brave and beautiful. Yes, there is always the risk that someone is less than tolerant and negatively judges you for being anxious. Their judgments of you say more about them than they do about you. Always. But most of the time you will be met with empathy and concern. Think about how you might respond if someone struggled with a panic attack in front of you. Even if you didn't personally experience anxiety, it is likely that you would feel care and concern toward that person rather than harsh judgements and negativity. If you *did* judge them for it, then again it would say more about *you* than it says about them!

Blocking beliefs can be difficult to challenge. They're often strong and intense, carrying a real fear of anxiety with them. Your progress through the E.A.S.E. Method depends on you working on these beliefs to change them so that you can accept anxiety (and all your emotional responses) and allow it to naturally subside. Challenging these beliefs starts with a decision to do so. You can decide that you no longer wish to perceive anxiety this way. Only then can you go about finding evidence for the new belief.

Have a look around you at people struggling with stuck anxiety. How many of them have become psychotic or been hospitalized against their will? How many people have died from a panic attack? And how many people have lost their ability to communicate because of anxiety? The more you question these blocking beliefs, the more you will see there is evidence that you will be able to cope and function just fine. Now is the time to actively look for the truth and begin to challenge any blocking beliefs you may have.

Time To Take Action

Using the Accept step is all about responding to anxiety differently. The next time anxiety shows up try the following steps:

- As you notice the anxiety breathe and create room for the symptoms to co-exist with you. Gently explore how anxiety feels in your body with curiosity. Try not to judge the symptoms as "bad' or "scary" but remain a neutral, curious observer.
- Say to yourself "this might feel uncomfortable, but it is not dangerous."
- For a brief moment consider the what if questions anxiety is throwing at you. Can you answer them and provide reassurance that you do have what it takes to cope with the unwanted outcomes?
- Think of anxiety as if it were a scared little child. What reassurance would this small child need from you? What can you say to your anxiety next time it flares up? Think of a few self-compassionate responses that you may use when you notice anxiety.
- Now stop focusing on what if questions and get present in this moment. What is true for you right now? Notice that you are safe in this moment.
- Can you identify any blocking beliefs? If yes, begin searching for facts and evidence that disproves the belief so that you may challenge the truth of it.

CHAPTER NINE

E.A.S.E. Step Three: Shift

Shift is a process that includes shifting your focus away from anxiety and back to the present moment, shifting any unhelpful beliefs and thoughts that generate anxiety, and shifting your life circumstances back into alignment with your true values, desires, and aspirations. Ultimately, by learning to shift your focus away from anxiety and toward your values, goals, and desires, you can cultivate positive emotions and experiences. This means you stop getting stuck in the vicious cycle of fear and overwhelm that comes when you fixate on your anxiety and its symptoms. Let's look at each layer of the Shift process.

Shift Your Focus

Shifting your focus away from anxiety and its symptoms to what you want is a powerful habit that you can cultivate with practice. You may have heard doctors, coaches, or therapists telling you to stop focusing on your anxiety. And you may have tried to make this shift without much success. So why is it so difficult to shift our focus when we're feeling anxious? Because the brain doesn't respond well to a negative command. *Don't think of a white elephant.* And there you go thinking about that elephant. *Don't eat all the chocolate biscuits.* And there you go putting your hand in the cookie jar.

Instead of saying "*Stop focusing on anxiety,*" let's say "*Pay more attention to....*" instead. You can practice focusing on anything that helps you feel calmer and more relaxed or keeps your mind occupied in a way that you enjoy or find useful. The aim is to get your eye off the anxiety and onto something more important. Now, some might say this is the same as using a distraction technique, and in some ways it might be. The difference is that we are not distracting ourselves from our anxiety because it is bad, dangerous, or scary. The goal is not to push the anxiety away. The intention here is simply to let it be and shift your focus onto something else. Release your tight grip on it and give it a chance to shift. So, no, this is not just a distraction. This is Shift.

I personally suggest you shift focus to the present moment. It is a simple shift you can implement anytime no matter where you are. Focusing on the present moment can help you get out of the anxiety loops and what if questions.

Think about it, anxiety rarely exists in the current moment. Except for health anxiety, which at times may focus on a current symptom as its source, most anxiety is rooted firmly in a possible unwanted outcome in the future or in worrying about a past mistake. In the present moment, there is often very little anxiety. When you become present, you can take stock of what is really happening and you'll be much better able to meet your need for safety.

Right here, right now, I am safe. I am running on time, I am appropriately dressed, I am healthy, and I am perfectly capable of doing what I am currently doing.

Once you answer all those what if questions, it is time to cast your attention back to the present moment and focus on what the facts are in this moment. You don't want to stay forever in a state of reassuring your anxiety, so it's time to move on. When you find yourself repeatedly checking your anxiety, stop yourself and focus on the present moment.

A great way to focus on this moment is the 5, 4, 3, 2, 1 exercise. You actively tell yourself to pause and notice your surroundings with your five senses.

- **What are five things you can see around you?** Are they bright, round, big, small? Pay attention to what you can see.
- **What are four things you can touch?** Notice what you feel in each object. Is it smooth, cold, rough, dry? Pay attention to what you feel.
- **What are three things you can hear?** Really listen and try to tune in to even the quietest sounds around you. What can you hear in the distance? Pay attention to what you hear.
- **What are two things you can smell?** Take a sniff and notice what you smell. If you are in public, feel free to take an inconspicuous sniff of your palm, your bag, or the air around you. Pay attention to what you smell.
- **What is one thing you can taste?** Taste something edible or take a sip of water. If nothing is available, simply notice any tastes or sensations in your mouth. Pay attention.

This strategy is incredibly powerful because it accomplishes two things. Not only does it focus your attention away from problematic thoughts and checking, but it also activates the pre-frontal cortex so you can think more rationally and objectively about the situation you're in. The rational brain and the emotional brain don't like to play together, so when one is active, the other tends to withdraw a little. This is largely why being in an anxious, emotional, or fight or flight state does not leave much room for rational, logical thought. When you force the rational brain into action, you also force the emotional brain to withdraw a little, and this calms your nervous system down.

The 5, 4, 3, 2, 1 strategy is also an excellent way to practice mindfulness. Remember that mindfulness is the act of paying attention to the present moment with curiosity and acceptance. You are simply observing what is around you with your five senses. It is important not to judge or evaluate what you see. Do not get caught in thoughts about the things you see being good or bad. Just observe and allow it to be. This practice strengthens your ability to continue leaning in to your experiences with acceptance and acknowledgment. Each step of the E.A.S.E. Method is teaching you an important skill, and these skills will strengthen and empower you as you practice them.

A Hobby for Your Mind

The Shift step is also a great opportunity to reinvest your time and energy into a hobby, new or old. Maybe your anxiety has gotten so bad that you have been avoiding certain activities or projects, so a great step in the right direction is to help reclaim these lost parts of yourself. Remember, you don't just want to tell your brain to stop looking at anxiety—that's the same as saying don't think about a white elephant. You need to practice directing your brain elsewhere, so any activity that requires active attention will be helpful to focus on.

Start thinking of all those interests and hobbies you once had that you have put aside in the interest of having kids, building a career, seeing to everyone else's needs, or focusing on anxiety. Shift is an opportunity to focus on taking good care of yourself again. Perhaps you used to paint or quilt. Maybe you enjoyed a hobby like photography, baking, or gardening. Consider the DIY project you never completed or the photobook you were going to put together. Write down a list of all your hobbies, past and present, and any potential hobbies you'd like to try.

As you become more involved in your old interests and hobbies, you will find less time available to fixate on the anxiety. Another transformation begins to happen. You begin to find yourself again, which means you slowly begin to build more confidence.

Shift Your Thoughts and Beliefs

We have explored how your thoughts and beliefs create and increase your anxiety. The Shift step also includes shifting these anxiety-provoking thoughts and putting you back in control of your mind. First, you must create some awareness of what you are thinking. What beliefs are you holding on to that contribute to your anxiety? As you have been reading, you may already become aware of some core beliefs or repetitive thoughts that create and maintain your anxiety. Perhaps you resonate with the Failure schema my husband struggled with or maybe you're a little more like myself and need everything to go according to plan, always putting pressure on yourself to perform. Many of my clients struggle with people pleasing and put their needs last in the service of others. Many of them also feel like they don't really fit in anywhere and experience social isolation. These beliefs are powerful in creating and maintaining anxiety and need to be addressed.

Here's the deal: Beliefs are like opinions. They are not truths or facts and you can change them at any time. You see, a fact can only be a fact if it is true 100% of the time. It is a fact that the sun rises in the east and sets in the west. There has never been a day that this has not happened. But when you begin to look at your beliefs, you will see that there are many instances in which the belief is not happening. My husband had numerous situations in which he excelled as a competent business owner despite the belief that he is a failure. Similarly, despite my unrelenting standards and the belief that something bad will happen if things don't go exactly according to plan, nothing terrible has ever happened. Even when things did not quite work out the way I expected them to, they still worked out just fine. It's just a belief that we need to be perfect in order to be ok. It's not truth.

And in the same way it is just a belief that you need to put the needs of others first in order to be loved and accepted. If you think back on your life, you will see there were times where you put your own needs first and others stuck around to support you. The truth is there is always someone who loves and accepts you. It's a belief that you cannot put your own needs first sometimes.

So where do these beliefs come from in the first place? Most of them were formed in your childhood when things were very different. They may have been useful in certain situations back then to help keep you safe. However, we know they are not true as adults because there is evidence against them. But beliefs are basically thoughts said on repeat enough times for us to begin believing them. And beliefs can change. The key is to find the thoughts that feed the belief and then begin to shift them. Create new thoughts that support the new belief you would like to have and emphasize these new thoughts over the old ones.

Cognitive Behavior Therapy is a useful tool in identifying and challenging unhelpful thoughts and beliefs. The first step is to become aware of what you are telling yourself on a regular basis. You cannot shift thoughts if you don't know what they are. The next step is to challenge these thoughts. It helps to remember that you are not your thoughts. Just because you think it doesn't make it true.

You are the thinker of your thoughts and, as such, you can decide what you want to think.

Shifting Your Thoughts Exercise

When an unhelpful, anxiety-provoking thought pops up stop and use one of the following techniques to challenge it. You can write down any anxious thoughts in a journal or use the free thought catching worksheet found on the resource page: www.theunstuckinitiative.com/giftofanxiety

Will I Buy This? Look at the thought as if it were for sale and ask yourself if you want to buy this thought. If you buy it, what will it cost you? For example, *I will lose control if I get anxious in public.* What does it cost you to buy into this thought? It likely means you won't go into public spaces, which stops you from going out with friends and family. It seems like a pretty expensive thought. Maybe you don't want to buy this one. Now consider what you would like to think or believe instead? Perhaps you're better off thinking *I've never really lost control when anxious and I have what it takes to move through an anxiety attack.* This thought comes with a very different feeling, doesn't it?

Cancel The Thought. Anxiety can throw all sorts of scary thoughts at you. When they pop up, imagine them as a pop-up box on your computer screen. Visualize that little X in the corner and click on it to cancel the thought the same way you would cancel the pop-up box.

Minimize The Thought: Some thoughts feel scary, loud, and ominous. You can take the power of those thoughts away by saying them in a funny voice that minimizes them. It might feel strange to do this but try saying the thought out loud in a squeaky voice that sounds silly. See if you can recognize the absurdity of the thought as you say it in this silly voice.

Focus on the Facts: The thoughts that create anxiety are rarely based in truth. They're imagined, unwanted outcomes that you feel anxious about experiencing. But when you return to the present you can ask yourself what the facts about the current situation are and whether they provide evidence for the thought you are having. If there is no evidence in this moment, then the thought is complete fiction, and you can let that go. Choose to focus on the facts. For example, you might worry about passing out when you become anxious in public. In this instance you are imagining a future unwanted outcome of fainting in front of others and feeling anxious about this. When you ask yourself what the facts are right now you will see that here, in this moment, you are not in a situation that is unsafe or anxiety-provoking. The only thing causing the anxiety is the idea of anxiety in the future. The facts right now are that you are safe and there is nothing in this moment to feel worried about.

The more you practice awareness and choice around your thoughts, the easier it becomes. The aim is always to put you back in control of your own mind rather than being at the mercy of anxious thoughts that are not based in reality!

Intrusive Thoughts

I often get asked about intrusive thoughts. Many clients feel afraid and overwhelmed by the intense, unwanted thoughts they have. Thoughts are classified as intrusive when they are intense, unwanted, and seem to come out of nowhere. These intrusive thoughts can include frightening content that may be violent, confusing, or gruesome. When struggling with stuck anxiety, your thoughts can become the source of more anxiety. Past clients have shared their fears that they may act on the thoughts they have or worry that the thoughts might mean something is deeply wrong with them. But these fears are unfounded.

The truth about intrusive thoughts is that we all have them from time to time. I have started logging my intrusive thoughts purely for the benefit of clients who worry whether it's normal to have intrusive thoughts. One day I was about to step into the road with my son before seeing a car that felt like it came out of nowhere. I got scared and stepped back but imagined myself taking the step with my son and throwing ourselves in front of the oncoming vehicle. The thought was vivid and included the gory details of being run over. It was disconcerting but I very quickly brushed it off and carried on with my day. Most of us have had experiences like this in one way or another. These intrusive thoughts are often intense and come with an uncomfortable feeling.

When we feel calm and our limbic brain is not running the show our rational brain has a chance to brush the thought off and move on without holding on to it. But if you're already feeling anxious and in a state of fight or flight, your emotional brain and amygdala is on the lookout for threats. A disconcerting thought like this could easily be misconstrued as threatening. *What if I really did jump in front of that car? What if I'm going crazy thinking like that?* Your anxious brain could be led into believing that this thought means something more sinister. And in this emotional state, you may begin to worry about whether you might act on these thoughts unwillingly.

The great news is that intrusive thoughts are still just thoughts. You can imagine going to the kitchen right now, grabbing an orange, and peeling it with a knife. You can think about eating that orange right now or even taking half of it and squishing it all over your face. Give it a go and think about it. While you are thinking about this orange and imagining it in as much graphic detail as possible, you are still sitting here reading this book. You have not, unwillingly, and unknowingly, gotten up and fetched an orange. You're not squishing it all over your face. That's because thoughts can only turn into behaviors if we put intentions behind them. Unless you intend to eat an orange and squish half of it on your face, your thought will remain just that a thought. And it is the same with intrusive thoughts.

This information is often enough to quell the anxiety generated by intrusive thoughts. The key is to remove the fear you have of the thought. The more you tell yourself not to think a certain way, the more that thought begins to pop up. What we resist always persists. The best thing to do when you experience an intrusive thought is to notice it and let it go. Do not make it mean anything more than it does and know that it can never become more than a thought without an intention behind it.

Shift Into Alignment

The Shift step requires a little more exploration. Sometimes anxiety is triggered by more than thoughts or beliefs. It can be a result of our lives feeling misaligned. At times, you might find yourself in situations that feel uncomfortable without knowing why. Perhaps your employer asked you to do something that doesn't feel ethically right to you. Maybe you are in a relationship that doesn't feel good, but you're not sure why. This is often when the life we are living, the job we find ourselves in, or the relationship we are investing energy in simply does not align with our values. When this occurs, then internal, psychic friction can happen, resulting in anxiety. The next phase of the Shift step helps to address these misalignments.

I often see a misalignment of values in my clients, which is unsurprising, really, because we simply do not talk much about values in our culture. Children aren't taught how to explore values in most schools or homes, and as adults we seldom think about our own values. While values are implicit, they are also powerful drivers of mental health.

Values are the ideas, concepts, and characteristics that we hold to be important and that contribute to us living a fulfilling life. They are more than morals. Values encompass who we want to be and what our purpose is. And they have a huge role to play in mental health. When you are living in alignment with your values, you will feel more content and fulfilled. You might feel like you are achieving something, progressing, or being a "good" person. However, when your life does not reflect your values, then things begin to feel uncomfortable, dissatisfying, and disappointing.

The issue is that we don't always know exactly what our values are, which can result in our lives being misaligned and our mental health deteriorating. Let's look at an example.

There are many people who value money, success, and achievement in their lives. Money is important to them because they value being a provider for their family and achieving financial stability. Working long hours feels satisfying, even though it takes them away from their families for longer periods of time. They are bringing in the money and providing financial stability. They feel fulfilled as they align with their values.

On the other hand, there are many people who really value connection, family, and altruism (selfless concern for the welfare of others). If they were placed in a similar corporate job earning lots of money and providing for their family, they might find themselves miserable and dissatisfied because they would not be living in alignment with their value of connection. They would likely prefer to work at a local charity organization and have significant time off to spend with their family.

Please note that there are no right or wrong values. Some values are not better than others. We value what we value.

However, sometimes we hold on to outdated values that no longer align with our own internal values. Maybe your family valued achievement and success. Your parents may have strived for financial security and pushed you to get a degree and a well-paying career so you could become successful. You may then find yourself in a high-end job, working long hours and feeling utterly miserable. If this resonates for you then you may end up anxious and stressed because you're living your life honoring the values from your family instead of your own internal values.

I have worked with many young adults who value adventure, connection with others, and self-discovery. They spend much of their time traveling and exploring the world. They are nearing their thirties and feeling the pressure to head home, get married, launch a career, and buy a house. And none of that resonates with their values. They feel stuck and anxious at the thought of doing what is expected of them because that would be abandoning their own values. When we make major life decisions based on other people's values, anxiety will come to warn us that something is off.

As you begin to shift your focus away from anxiety and toward a life you wish to live, you should explore your values and feelings about your life and realign areas that feel out of balance for you.

Time To Take Action

Now is the time to practice shifting. There are two ways you can shift your focus away from anxiety and its symptoms:

- The first is to shift your focus away from anxiety and onto something new. What will you be focusing on? Grab a piece of paper and brainstorm a list of all your hobbies past and present. Now add some activities or hobbies you have an interest in trying. Pick the top two activities you're interested in and schedule time to begin them this month. This sets you up with something new to focus on any time you need to take your eye off anxiety and onto something else.
- Practice bringing your attention to the present moment. Use the 54321 exercise and find:
  - 5 things you can see,
  - 4 things you can touch,
  - 3 things you can hear,
  - 2 things you can smell and
  - 1 thing you can taste.

Remember to simply observe what you see without judgement.

Shifting Unhelpful Thoughts Exercise

When your thoughts are spiraling and causing more anxiety, use the following exercises to begin separating from those thoughts and taking back control:

- Use the thought catching worksheet on the resource page www.theunstuckinitiative.com/giftofanxiety to create awareness of your repetitive and anxiety-provoking thoughts.
- Using your new awareness of repetitive and anxiety-provoking thoughts, what negative beliefs might you hold about yourself? It may be helpful to write down any beliefs that these thoughts might be pointing to. Now consider what beliefs you would prefer to hold about yourself? What new thoughts could you be having that would support these new beliefs? Feel free to use your journal to explore what comes up for you.
- Use one of the 4 strategies to shift negative, unwanted thoughts:
  - Would I Buy That?
  - Cancel The Thought
  - Minimize The Thought
  - What Are the Facts?

Values Alignment Exercise

It is time to evaluate our values and see whether we are living in alignment, or possibly need to shift.

You may want to use the Values Exploration sheet and Values Exercise found on the online resource page at www.theunstuckinitiative.com/giftofanxiety . The Values Exploration sheet includes clear instructions to help you identify your current values as well as any inherited values. You may then use the Values Exercise to identify specific areas in your life that may be misaligned and in need of attention. As you begin to shift your focus off the anxiety you now have clear ideas on where to focus your attention and energy in a way that aligns with your values.

CHAPTER TEN

E.A.S.E. Step Four: Engage

The fourth phase of stuck anxiety is avoidance. Avoidance intensifies anxiety by signaling that the thing you're avoiding must be dangerous if you're avoiding it. The more you avoid, the stronger the anxiety gets. The idea that you will reduce anxiety by avoiding things is a con that avoidance and anxiety have you believing in. Avoidance is a cheap, temporary solution that creates long-term problems. The fourth step of the E.A.S.E. Method, Engage, is a direct antidote to avoidance.

We've discussed how you may feel a strong urge to avoid the outcome of your what if questions. The anxiety tells you that you need to be safe, and it tells you that avoidance is the way to do that. *Just cancel. Do it tomorrow when you are feeling better. You won't cope. You're too anxious. You're not confident enough.*

Remember Shameful Submission is when you give in to your anxiety and give up whatever your goal was by avoiding the situation. Imagine if all those anxious thoughts were actually the things your friends and family were telling you. Of course you would feel like crap about yourself. Of course you would want to stay home. Of course you would continue feeling anxious. When you give in to your urges to avoid things in life, you confirm to your anxiety that all those statements are indeed true. You begin to shamefully submit to the false statements that anxiety has you believing. Even if Shameful Submission is not your primary response to anxiety, avoidance will likely still be present. It is the primary coping mode used by people with stuck anxiety. The more you avoid, the more defeated you feel, and the vicious cycle of stuck anxiety continues!

This is why most therapists and anxiety programs encourage exposure. The theory is that you do the thing you feel afraid of to show yourself (and your anxiety) that there was nothing to fear. Once you have exposed yourself to the anxiety-provoking task a few times, the fear should subside as you create the new belief that you are, indeed, safe. However, some people try exposures and end up feeling more anxious than before. This is largely because they felt intense anxiety during the experience, didn't know how to cope with it, and then opted out mid-way. When you opt out midway you confirm to your brain that the task or action is, indeed, dangerous and that you can't possibly follow through with it. Of course, this trains your brain to generate more anxiety the next time you want to give it a try.

While I completely understand the theory and logic behind exposures, I also understand that you need the right foundation before facing your biggest fears. As you read this, you might not feel ready to let go of avoidance. You may still be afraid of experiencing anxiety. In fact, the belief that is strongest at keeping anxiety stuck is the belief that you cannot cope with being anxious. It is also the belief that drives the avoidance. That is why we have the first three steps before heading into the Engage step. However, by the time you enter the fourth step of the E.A.S.E. Method, you will have already gained back confidence and the ability to be with and tolerate anxiety, and you will have started looking up once again.

The Upward Cycle of Wellbeing

Most people I work with complain that their lives have become smaller as they restrict more areas of their lives due to anxiety. They say that they wish their lives could go back to being bigger than the anxiety and that they could say yes to more experiences. Unfortunately, their fear and avoidance has created very specific areas of safety that tend to get smaller the more they avoid.

Perhaps you also have an imaginary line a specific distance from your home that you're too anxious to cross. There is no real reason why it feels unsafe to pass that point, but anxiety says it is too far and you'll get too anxious so you never go beyond it. That's how life gets smaller and your confidence diminishes. Naturally we want to undo this. Engage is the process by which you begin to regain confidence and expand your comfort zone.

Maybe your anxious thoughts are already popping up. *But I am not ready. I must gain more confidence, and then I'll do it.* The thing about confidence is that it doesn't grow while you wait for it. Confidence grows when you stretch yourself a little out of your comfort zone and then show yourself what you are capable of. Confidence grows as you learn new things. You learned all about anxiety in step one. You gained knowledge and confidence. Now, it is time to act.

It is only through action that you will grow your confidence and create an upward spiral of wellbeing. You see, the more you say yes to doing the things that feel a little anxiety provoking, the more confidence you will gain. You will begin to realize that you are capable of so much more than anxiety had you believing, which will leave you feeling more empowered and more capable of accepting anxiety and facing situations you have been avoiding. As you become more empowered and accepting of anxiety, you will naturally stop all the excessive self-monitoring of your symptoms as you shift your focus toward your goals. You will begin to engage more and build more confidence. This is how you can turn the downward spiral of the anxiety loop into the upward cycle of wellness one step at a time.

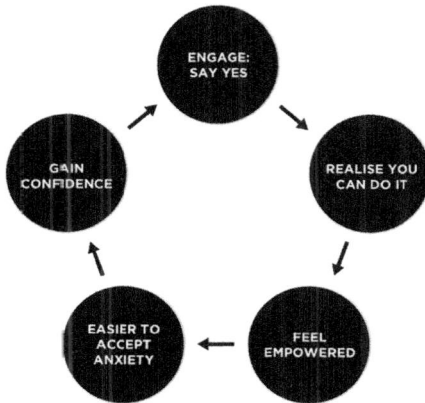

Small Steps To Saying Yes

The Engage step requires you to start by saying yes to one small thing you have been avoiding. The key here is to start small. The last thing we want is for you to dive headfirst into the deep end only to find it deeper than you imagined and more traumatizing than it needed to be. So start small and build on one positive step after another.

At this point it is useful to get clear about what, exactly, you have been avoiding and what that has cost you in the process. Remember that the brain has stored avoidance as the go-to coping strategy due to rewards-based learning. The only way you can undo this is by showing your brain that avoidance does not bring rewards. A great proverb shared by motivational speaker Les Brown explains why. The story goes that there was a young man walking down the street who saw an old man sitting on his porch. Next to the old man was his dog, who was whining and whimpering. The young man asked the old man "What's wrong with your dog?" The old man explained that the dog was lying on a nail. The young man wondered why the dog wouldn't just get up and move. The old man replied that the dog was old with arthritis and moving was more painful than just staying on the nail. In short, the nail wasn't hurting him bad enough to move. Humans are much the same. We will only make a change when the pain of staying the same outweighs the pain of changing. This means that you will only stop avoiding things when the avoidance feels more painful to you than facing your anxiety and taking action. Here's an example to illustrate this point.

I am not a fan of making phone calls to people I don't know. I would much rather write an email than talk on the phone. On some level, I am irrationally worried that I won't know what to say or will sound stupid, and these thoughts stir up my anxiety. I prefer to use online booking systems to arrange medical appointments or make restaurant reservations. And it normally works out just fine unless there is no online system for booking, which means I need to pick up the phone and make a call.

When I realized the online booking system was not available to book my dentist appointment, I promptly pushed organizing an appointment to the bottom of my to-do list for the day. "I'll call after lunch," I said to myself. I found excuses for after lunch and then put it off to tomorrow. As with most cases of avoidance, however, tomorrow never came. Not even when the tooth in question began to bother me at night. I couldn't make the call that late at night anyway so I would promise myself to call first thing in the morning.

Morning would come, the toothache a memory, and I conveniently forgot to call the dentist. It took six weeks for me to finally make the appointment. Thankfully, there were no significant repercussions. However, I had endured six weeks of persistent pain and worry about my tooth, as well as random midnight anxious nudges to make the call. This additional worry and anxiety could have been avoided completely had I just picked up the phone to call the dentist the first time.

While this example may seem small in comparison to some of the bigger things you find yourself avoiding, you will likely notice similar behaviors in your own story like putting it off, promising yourself you'll do it later, and how the longer you avoid the situation the harder it seems to be to get yourself to take action. Your anxiety keeps cropping up in some way or another to remind you to get to it, but you keep avoiding it. The anxiety never really goes away when you keep avoiding the situation, does it?

The only real way to remove the anxiety is by facing the issue head on. Perhaps it is a call to a family member or friend you have been putting off. Maybe a work project that you have been pushing aside. You may be avoiding an event or get together, saying next time to the same group of people who keep asking you to join them. Perhaps you are saying tomorrow to your own self-care, such as exercise or a boundary you want to put in place with someone.

If the brain thinks there is a reward for avoidance (relief from anxiety) it will continue to ask you to avoid. So instead, let's flip the script. First, you need to identify what the avoidance is costing you. When you clearly identify the cost, then you undo the sense of reward that the brain believes it gets from avoidance. You and your brain become aware of how avoidance is, in fact, causing more of a problem. I suggest you spend some time writing a list of all the activities and decisions you have been avoiding. Try to be as honest as possible with yourself. And remember that thoughts like "I don't have time right now" or "I can just do this tomorrow" are just perpetuating the avoidance. You can flip the script by asking, "What if I do have time right now?"

Once you have written down your list, let's get real about what each case of avoidance has cost you. In my case, it cost me six weeks of midnight toothache and low-level anxiety to get things done. In other cases, it might be costing you relationships, money, health, and wellbeing. Try to be as specific as you can about the costs involved. We really want the brain to recognize the avoidance as doing more harm than good.

Once you create your list, you can begin to identify areas where you will start engaging again. It is very important to start with small, achievable steps. With small and achievable steps, you ensure that each action is a confirmation of your ability so you can gain more confidence. As you take those initial steps, you will begin to prove through experience that engaging is a rewarding activity, and you will disprove any negative, anxiety-related beliefs about your perceived inability to cope or do things.

There are two phases to the Engage step: Intentions and Celebrations.

Setting Intentions

Intentions are really goals, but I prefer to call them intentions. Goals imply that we have failed if we did not achieve them, whereas intentions provide a buffer if we aren't able to follow through. Remember that self-compassion is a key ingredient in any step of the E.A.S.E. Method, and it is no different here. We understand that life can get in the way of our best intentions and that does not mean we have failed. It simply means that life got in the way.

Intentions are necessary to guide where we are headed, and when we set S.M.A.R.T. intentions, then we have a recipe for success with Engage. The acronym S.M.A.R.T. was coined by George Doran, Arthur Miller, and James Cunningham in their 1981 article "There's a S.M.A.R.T. way to write management goals and objectives." S.M.A.R.T. intentions are:

- Specific
- Measurable
- Achievable
- Relevant
- Time sensitive

Now, as you look through the list of things you have been avoiding, begin to identify an area that feels most relevant to begin working with. Maybe it is the area that has cost you the most. Or perhaps it is simply the area that feels easiest to begin with. There is no right or wrong here; simply choose what feels most relevant. You are now going to create an intention in that area. Perhaps it is that phone call you need to make, a self-care activity, or scheduling that dance class you've been thinking about.

We are going to apply the S.M.A.R.T. principles to this intention to make your intention clear and more achievable. Having clear intentions helps you stay focused on taking the next step and achieving a goal instead of feeling stuck because you don't know what the next step is.

Remember that the E.A.S.E. Method is designed to help you remove your fear of anxiety. This means that you are learning how to be with anxiety instead of pushing it away and you are learning how to take back control instead of letting anxiety make your decisions for you. The idea here is to do something with or without anxiety, but being anxiety-free is not the outcome you are striving for. The outcome is simply doing it and the goal is to show yourself that you can do things regardless of whether you feel anxious or not. When you can prove to your brain that anxiety cannot harm you, terrify you, or make you lose control, then you gain more confidence to do more things. For this very reason, the intentions you set need to be achievable. You may look at them and think "this is not enough. I should be doing more" but please start small and do not undermine your achievements. Your success depends on you making progress one step at a time. Here are a few examples to illustrate this point.

Examples of S.M.A.R.T. Engage intentions:

One of the things Anna began avoiding was going on bike rides because she didn't feel confident to go out on her own and believed she would become anxious when doing so. During the Engage step, her intention was to do more bike rides in the week ahead. But Anna's goal was not specific. Where would she go for her bike ride? What time? How long would she go for? And how many times in the upcoming week was she aiming to go for a ride? As she narrowed down the specifics of her intention, she was able to create more clarity.

Anna realized that a long bike ride would probably feel overwhelming, so she decided to start with a short ride around the neighborhood. This felt familiar, safe and, most importantly, achievable. She planned out the specific route. She also recognized that the weather could deter her, so achieving a specified number of rides for the upcoming week might not be possible. Anna decided she would ride at least once, since chances were the weather would be good at least one day of the week, and she would do so on the first day of appropriate weather conditions.

Now her intention was specific, measurable, and attainable. It was relevant because Anna missed her bike rides and knew that the exercise, fresh air, and getting out there again would contribute to her sense of wellbeing. It was time sensitive in that she had one week to complete it. And most importantly, Anna knew she was going to take the bike-ride with or without anxiety. She returned the following week having been on three bikes rides. She had enjoyed the first one so much that she set out on a longer one for the next two. She also expressed her sheer enjoyment in having prioritized herself. She felt so good about herself and her new habit of riding that she began to set new intentions in other areas of life as well. She was learning to let go of her fixation with anxiety and shift her focus to meeting her needs once again.

Another client, Lydia, came to me stuck in a vicious cycle of anxiety. She worried that she would have a panic attack while driving and then lose control and be unable to get herself home. This fear about her anxiety caused her to avoid driving alone. She was desperate to regain her independence. so she set an intention of going for a drive during the week. We needed to get more specific and make the intention highly attainable. Lydia agreed that driving to the end of her road and back home again would be achievable. She decided to do so on the following Tuesday morning at 10 am (when morning traffic had subsided). She now had a specific, measurable, attainable, relevant, and time sensitive goal.

Lydia was aware that she would likely be very anxious while taking action on her intention. She never expected the outcome to be an anxiety-free drive. The goal was for her to take her anxiety along for the ride and show herself that she could remain in control while driving.

Lydia achieved this goal and then went on to set longer drives as future intentions. Each time she carried through with her intention, she showed herself that she was capable of coping with anxiety. By learning to accept that fact that she may experience anxiety or even a panic attack, her anxiety was able to subside. She was learning to let go of her old patterns of Nervous Control.

These examples serve to illustrate how important it is to set small and attainable intentions when you begin. Those initial steps are needed to build confidence and show the brain how possible it is for you to get out there and say yes again. Remember to focus on how rewarding it feels to take action so you can train your brain to feel good again and undo the cycle of avoidance. Acknowledge yourself for taking action in spite of your anxiety. Tell yourself you're making progress because you are! As you recognize the cost of avoidance and couple that knowledge with the reward of engaging in new habits, you're well on your way to undoing the fourth phase of stuck anxiety.

Time for Celebrations

As soon as you follow through on your first intention, it's time to start celebrating your success. No matter how small you think the intention was, the fact is you set it and went about achieving it. This is a big improvement compared to where you have been—stuck in a cycle of anxiety and avoidance. Let's celebrate it.

Many clients struggle with this because they don't see their accomplishments as big enough to celebrate. They say things like "everyone else can do this, so why should I celebrate this?" or "I used to be able to do this so it's not that big of a deal." Most of the time they believe they should be further than they are.

I love the concept of the gap and the gain introduced by Dan Sullivan and Dr. Benjamin Harvey.[9] Most people evaluate themselves based on the ideal version of themselves. They look at how they are performing and measure it up against the ideal of how they wish to be performing. This is the gap. And there will always be a gap because, for most of us, the ideal version is the perfect version. The one that is unattainable. Instead, we really should be measuring ourselves based on how far we have come. This is the gain. The amount of progress we have made since a previous point in our own immediate history. Think about yourself and the trajectory of your anxiety. How much progress have you made when you follow through on your intention and do it, even while anxious? Please measure yourself based on how far you have come rather than the gap between where you are and where you wish to be. Measuring against the gain always builds confidence because you can see your progress. Measuring against the gap can leave you feeling inadequate.

When you Celebrate your successes you build a deep sense of validation and approval. You do not always need to receive validation and approval from others. Luckily, you can validate and appreciate yourself, and that experience can help ease your anxiety and cultivate confidence. Celebrations need not be extravagant. You do not need to host a small party, spend money, or make a big fanfare. Celebrations can be as simple as giving yourself a pat on the back or verbally acknowledging yourself for a job well done.

I find that doing a little happy dance while singing, "I did it, I did it!" feels great for me. It's even more powerful when you do that with someone else and share the celebration. When another person witnesses your success and you acknowledge it out loud to someone else, it can help you feel seen and understood for your progress. Consider sharing your wins with your closest friends and family when you first start out.

Celebrations are also a powerful way to reinforce the reward for achieving your intention. Because your brain uses reward-based learning, it will create urges for you to repeat an action if there was a positive outcome and reward. When you celebrate following through on your intentions, then your brain feels the reward and will become more motivated to do work on your intention again next time.

Too often, I am faced with clients who did not celebrate their wins because they couldn't think of anything to do at the time. It helps to be prepared and know what you will do in advance.

The smallest of celebrations count if you are doing them with the intention of acknowledging your win. You can make use of preplanned events as celebrations if you state that the event (going out for dinner, having a friend over, taking time to read your book uninterrupted) is going to be part of your celebration. When you feel like your accomplishments are being acknowledged, seen, and understood, you will feel a sense of excitement and mental wellbeing. Today it might just be a five-minute drive, but before you know it you'll be on a road trip with your best friend having more fun than you've had in years.

As you complete your first engage intention and celebration, head back to your list and set the next one. This is a process that you keep repeating as you take small, attainable steps toward regaining confidence and building your mental wellbeing.

Time To Take Action

The first step is to gain clarity on your specific avoidance and the cost thereof. Write a list of all the activities and decisions you have been avoiding. Then go through the list and carefully consider what avoiding each one has cost you.

Now pick one area to start with and create a S.M.A.R.T. intention to reengage with life in a way that's more aligned with your true values.

Here are some questions to ask yourself regarding your next intention:

- Is it specific enough? Can you identify when, how, where, and for how long you will be completing this intention?
- Is it measurable? How will you know that you have achieved your intention?
- Is it attainable? Ask yourself if there is anything at all that could get in the way of you achieving this intention. It is helpful to rate how likely it is that you will achieve it out of 10 (10 being an absolute certainty). If your number is not at least a 9, then ask yourself why and adjust the specificity or reduce the expectation to bring the rating to a 9.
- Is it relevant? How does it help you or move you forward? What will you gain by achieving this intention?
- Is it time sensitive? Have you given yourself a specific time frame in which to complete your intention?

Begin by setting just one intention for the week ahead using the S.M.A.R.T. principles. Then see how you feel after accomplishing that one step.

After completing your intention, make sure to celebrate your win! No matter how small you think it may be, now is the time to acknowledge your effort and achievements.

Consider where you were before you followed through on your intention and consider how far you have come with this small step. Remember to evaluate your progress against the gain and not the gap.

Write down some ideas for ways you can celebrate your achievements that would feel good to you whether it's sharing your accomplishment with a friend, doing a little happy dance, or telling yourself you did a great job. Commit to following through with the celebration too.

CHAPTER ELEVEN

Putting Together the Four Steps

When starting out with the E.A.S.E. Method, either as a framework or as a step-by-step process, it is best to work through the steps in chronological order. Each step creates a foundation for the next step to take place, and the method builds upon itself. It is important to feel empowered and confident enough to accept anxiety as a valid emotional response that cannot harm you and will subside. Only once you can accept anxiety and tolerate it will you be able to shift your focus and let it go. The fourth step follows once you can let anxiety go and engage with more challenges and opportunities in life.

While the E.A.S.E. Method is a clear, four-step process, it is not necessarily a process with a clear end. It is not a method that, implemented once, will end stuck anxiety once and for all. The E.A.S.E. Method is a new perspective that allows you to respond to anxiety with Empowered Acceptance. The steps described here will help you create a new understanding of anxiety that changes the way you feel about it and behave toward it. You will need to follow each step in detail to create the necessary change in your understanding. But once you have laid the foundation for your new response you will be able to respond to future (inevitable) anxiety with E.A.S.E. and ensure that it doesn't become stuck again.

This is how my husband now responds to his anxiety when it shows up and it has prevented stuck anxiety from coming back despite the many challenges we have faced since that difficult year. The Empowered Acceptance response is implemented swiftly and immediately when anxiety shows up. You simply ask yourself what anxiety is asking you to pay attention to and, because you've already done the work of answering "why me?" and "why now?" and identified your core beliefs, finding this answer will be much easier in the future. Immediately you acknowledge and accept the anxiety. It makes sense now that you understand it so you take a deep breath and create space for it to exist within you. Simply let it be wherever you feel it in your body. However, it is important that you also shift your focus away from it. With this new response you do not make the anxiety mean anything more than it does. You do not over-evaluate the symptoms or keep checking it. You just let it be and keep engaging in your life in the present moment. You speak to yourself with greater self-compassion and acceptance and say things like; *Yes, I am feeling anxious now and that's okay. I'm just going to focus on getting ready for the day instead of worrying about what might happen if we're late. I can deal with that later if it happens at all.*

That is how you promptly respond to ordinary anxiety when it shows up.

Sometimes anxiety sticks around a little longer than you like. Each time you notice it, you respond with these four steps: (1) Acknowledge and pay attention, (2) Accept and let it be there, (3) shift your focus back to the present, and (4) keep doing what you're doing. If you notice it repeatedly returning then it means there is something that still needs attention. It may be the core belief that is no longer serving you. It could be that you need to give yourself more self-compassion and self-care. As you'll see in the following chapters, anxiety is often alerting you to important areas in your life that are no longer serving you and need to change. If they stay the same, anxiety will keep ringing the alarm until you make changes that help you feel safe. That is how anxiety becomes your greatest ally.

Time To Take Action

Many clients need reminders of what to do when their anxiety pops up. You can create little reminders to stick on your fridge or bathroom mirror to remind you of the four steps to an Empowered Acceptance response.

1. Acknowledge the anxiety and pay attention. Answer "why me?" and "why now?"
2. Breathe and create space for anxiety. Give yourself permission to feel this way. Answer any what if questions.
3. Shift your focus off the anxiety back to the present. What is true for you in this moment?
4. Get back to what you were doing with all of your focus and attention.

CHAPTER TWELVE

Listening to What Anxiety Is Telling You

"I feel dread at the start of everyday. So anxious I can't even get out of bed. I just want to go back to sleep, but of course I can't fall asleep again, so I lie there tossing and turning with all this anxiety."

This is how Nora described her experience of anxiety the first time I met her. She had no idea why she was waking up anxious every morning. She decided she needed help finding a way to deal with the anxiety that almost paralyzed her at the start of her day.

Once a personal assistant to a prestigious CEO at a large company, Nora had since been made redundant, which forced her into a job selling commercial properties. She described herself as previously confident and ambitious. However, the situation leading to her redundancy had left her feeling inadequate and doubting her own abilities. Nevertheless, Nora made a real go of it with her new position and was relatively successful at selling commercial property. She earned a good living off her commissions and thought she would enjoy the freedom and flexibility that working from home brought her.

But soon Nora found herself pressing snooze on her alarm, losing motivation, and experiencing an increase in morning anxiety. She said she had never felt much anxiety before, so she was baffled by the creeping nerves each morning. Day after day, she found herself avoiding getting out of bed and dreading the day ahead. Nora found it difficult to understand why she was feeling so anxious in the morning and why the anxiety would go away later in the day.

Most people feel at least a little confused about their anxiety. Unless there is a very clear situation resulting in nerves and worry, most stuck anxiety has become pervasive, distracting, and confusing. Understanding that anxiety always pops up for a reason and then exploring what that reason may be helps you regain control and puts you in a position to meet the need that anxiety is alerting you to.

Four Reasons for Anxiety (Answering Why Now)

In my experience there are normally 4 reasons for anxiety showing up at a particular time. Remember that reasons answer the "why now?" question. You will find that anxiety is often caused by one or more of the following:

1. A core belief that has been triggered
2. A past trauma that has been triggered.
3. You're avoiding something.
4. Your system is stressed.

Let's discuss these in more detail.

When a Core Belief Gets Triggered

This is one of the most common reasons anxiety crops up unexpectedly. When you find yourself wondering why the current, seemingly safe situation has you strung up with butterflies and a racing heart, chances are a core belief or trauma has been triggered. This was the case with my husband and the run-in he had with the builder at work. The situation that ensued had triggered my husband's impostor syndrome and core belief that he was a failure, resulting in his anxious brain screaming at him to pay attention and fix the problem before he lost it all.

Core beliefs can be both positive and negative. The negative ones are rarely accurate. The ones that trigger anxiety—or other distressing emotional responses—are generally based on false lessons learned during childhood. The most common negative core beliefs, some of which may resonate with you, include:

- I'm not good enough.
- I need to be perfect to be valued.
- I'm too much/ I'm a burden.
- I'm weak / stupid.
- Bad things happen to me.

While you may not be overtly aware of your own core beliefs, they will tend to influence your behavior and your expectations of the world around you. For example, if someone holds the core belief that others cannot be trusted, they will tend to hold people at arm's length and expect to be taken advantage of. In the same way, if someone holds the belief that they are too much or a burden, they may be less assertive about their own needs. In fact, they may find themselves actively pleasing others and ensuring that the people around them are happy before meeting their own needs. They might expect others to feel annoyed if they ask for help themselves and believe they will be perceived as needy or demanding if they give voice to their own preferences.

Core beliefs are formed through early experiences with significant caregivers (such as parents, family, and teachers) throughout our childhood. These beliefs are created as we learn how to find acceptance, belonging, and approval. For example, growing up in a culture where "children should be seen and not heard" creates adults that become people pleasers, who believe their own needs are too much or too demanding.

Most core beliefs have been formed to ensure your safety and acceptance. They are born from experiences in which your safety was jeopardized in some way, and your amygdala stored the experience in the "never to be repeated" basket.

For example, when your caregivers high fived you for your achievements and showed disappointment when you missed the mark, a belief that you always need to perform well may have been created. Your brain recognized the displeasure in your caregivers and, wanting you to remain acceptable and ensure your survival, your brain created the theory that you need to continue doing well to remain lovable. Your safety is thus ensured when you perform at your best and anything less than your best becomes a risk to your acceptance and, therefore, your survival (at least according to your primitive brain). This is how the core belief of Unrelenting Standards is created.

How does this result in anxiety later in life? Remember, most people are not aware of their core beliefs. They simply go about their daily lives being subconsciously influenced by these operating principles until something happens in their lives to trigger the belief. My husband's experience is a prime example.

When the core belief has been triggered, the brain thinks that survival has somehow been threatened. The core belief that he was a failure, and thus shouldn't try anything new, was activated when he started his own business. My husband experienced low-level anxiety throughout that time in his life. That core belief was then fully triggered when the builder called his workmanship into question. As the core belief was triggered, his brain started screaming that acceptance, approval, and his survival was threatened, and it was all going to come crumbling down around him.

My anxiety is often triggered by my unrelenting standards and core beliefs like "I have to get it right or else I'll be in trouble." This tends to be one of my main operating schemas and means that I feel enormous pressure to perform perfectly every time. Failure and mistakes are simply not an option to me when this core belief is in action. I know many of you resonate with this, as it seems to be a common core belief among those who struggle with anxiety. This means that when life throws curve balls at people with this schema and things don't go exactly according to plan, the core belief is triggered, and a sense that it is all going to fall apart ensues. Cue anxiety.

Even in writing this book, I experience anxiety about getting it out into the world. I need to get it right and it must be perfect or else. *Or else what?* I ask my anxiety. This core belief states that if things aren't perfect, exactly right, then you're not good enough and you will be rejected. Cue anxiety.

Emotional Inhibition is another very common core belief I see in the clients I work with. This core belief says that showing emotions and being vulnerable in front of others is unsafe because they may judge you negatively, reject you, or get angry with you. Emotional Inhibition normally shows up in families where feelings and mental health were not commonly discussed or shared. Parents may have been too busy or uncomfortable to talk about big, messy feelings and worked hard to keep their emotions calm or hidden. This type of environment often creates two main patterns. First, children don't learn how to regulate their own feelings because no one showed them how to soothe themselves. So these children grow up believing that big, uncomfortable feelings are unsafe and intolerable. Secondly, they grow up believing that other people won't know what to do with their feelings either and will likely react negatively to them if they did show their emotions.

This perpetuates stuck anxiety. Why? Because the anxiety or panic becomes the emotional response that feels unsafe and intolerable, which means that people with the Emotional Inhibition core belief will try everything to push anxiety (and other feelings) away to make them stop. They're afraid of showing their anxiety to other people, which drives the fear of becoming anxious or having a panic attack in public. With Emotional Inhibition core belief, each experience of anxiety becomes the threat that anxiety wants you to pay attention to.

Working with Core Beliefs and Anxiety

The good news is we can learn to understand and shift our core beliefs. They are not set in stone. It was during a coaching session that Nora explored her feelings toward her job and working from home. On the face of it, she should have felt blessed that she was able to generate an income despite the economic upheaval of the pandemic. She had a job that could just as easily be conducted from the comfort of her home office as anywhere else without affecting her income. For all intents and purposes, Nora should have felt happy and content.

And yet, as we explored her values and core beliefs, she realized she felt deeply miserable at her job. Not only was the work from home situation extremely isolating, but she also harbored her own unrelenting standards of herself and held a core belief that said she needed to be working harder and more efficiently. When you have spent much of your adult life believing that hard work means working a forty-hour week at an office with clearly delineated job tasks, setting your own work hours from a home office can feel like you're being lazy. Holding on to core beliefs like unrelenting standards can also get in the way of giving yourself grace and allowing yourself to be more flexible with your work habits.

With deeper exploration, Nora admitted that she worried about her income, which was commission based. While she knew she was a capable agent, she still carried beliefs that she was not good enough. She had been made redundant at her past job, after all. How could she have faith in her abilities now? Nora was afraid she would not be able to sell another property and, therefore, not make the required income to continue her lifestyle.

As Nora began to listen to her anxiety, coupled with an exploration of her core beliefs and values, she began to realize that she dreaded the day ahead because she felt she was not capable of making a success of it. She harbored beliefs that she wasn't working hard enough and feared that she would fall short on making the income she needed. No small wonder her anxiety was screaming at her every morning!

As she became aware of the core beliefs being triggered, Nora was able to address the pressure she was putting on herself and challenge the belief that she was not good enough.

Kath is another great example of working through core beliefs to shift stuck anxiety. She contacted me after a significant panic attack that left her agoraphobic and too afraid to leave her home. Kath was adamant that she had never experienced anxiety before this event, but on deeper exploration she was able to recognize signs of stress that she had been brushing aside for years. Kath experienced her first panic attack when she returned to her car after visiting a Covid-19 testing center. As she readied herself for the hour-long commute home she suddenly experienced all the usual symptoms of panic, including chest pain, dizziness, and being convinced there was something terribly wrong with her. Petrified, she called her husband who helped her get to the hospital for a checkup. Kath's medical evaluation came back normal and she was sent home with a diagnosis of anxiety.

Kath reached out to me because she could not tolerate the thought of another panic attack. She stayed home all day scrutinizing every sign and symptom in her body desperately trying to avoid another attack. The more anxious she felt, the more symptoms she saw and the more afraid she would become of having another panic attack.

She was unable to get in her car, leave her home, or return to work. The reason anxiety became stuck was because her Emotional Inhibition core belief had been triggered. Kath could not tolerate the intensity of the anxiety and kept telling herself it was unsafe. She could not even think about taking that anxiety into public lest she have a panic attack in front of others. A keen participant in my program, Kath worked hard at changing her response.

She felt enormous relief when she finally gave herself permission to feel anxious. Identifying the core belief, she bravely put herself out there to challenge the idea that others would judge her for feeling anxious. Even though she was nervous about sharing her anxiety, she told her vet she may need to leave during the consult due to a panic attack. Unsurprisingly, her anxiety reared during the consult and Kath was met with empathy and kindness, challenging the belief that others would react negatively. Taking this a step further, Kath eventually returned to work, bravely informing her employer and colleagues that she may feel anxious at times. By acknowledging it to others, Kath was inadvertently accepting her anxiety and herself, which stopped the vicious cycle of anxiety about anxiety. With each step of Engaging, she undid the belief that her emotional experiences were intolerable, unsafe, and unacceptable to others. Since then, Kath has taken bigger and braver steps with anxiety. She has attended the dentist, sat in an auditorium for her son's graduation, been on a road-trip with her husband, and flown to Florida for a vacation.

As you identify the core beliefs that are being triggered and causing anxiety you will inadvertently create more compassion toward yourself and the anxiety you feel. As a result, it feels less frightening and much easier to tolerate.

When Trauma is Triggered

When you've had past traumatic experiences where your safety was clearly threatened, current situations that look and feel similar may trigger the amygdala to sound the alarm and get you to pay attention. Both Little T and Big T traumas may trigger anxiety.

Post-Traumatic Stress Disorder vs. Stuck Anxiety

Many people who have suffered Big-T trauma will find their amygdala is working very hard to keep them safe. It has become hypervigilant and believes almost anything could be a threat. The anxiety is on alert because the brain is persistently ringing anxious alarm bells as it desperately tries to keep you safe from a repeat of the trauma previously experienced. If you experience flashbacks or random, unwanted recollections of the trauma as well as significant avoidance and changes in your mood then the anxiety you feel likely forms part of a post-traumatic stress response. This anxiety is different from stuck anxiety because you are not necessarily anxious about being anxious. While you may feel anxious most of the time, this anxiety is predominantly a result of a stressed and traumatized brain and an overactive watchdog.

The E.A.S.E. Method is still useful in listening to the anxiety and identifying the reason, which in this case would be past unresolved trauma. You would still use many of the concepts explained in this book to prevent becoming anxious about your anxiety. However, you would likely find additional relief from trauma therapy directed at helping you and your brain process the unresolved trauma and associated beliefs and feelings.

Little T Trauma and Stuck Anxiety

Most people, if not all, would have experienced some childhood events that felt traumatic at the time. And while you may not think of those events as traumatic in the traditional sense of the word, the events would have been disruptive or upsetting and will have added to your perspective of yourself and the world. These Little T traumas may have included disruptions to your relationship with your caregivers, such as a parent passing away, divorce, or serious illness. You may have had experiences of bullying, major life transitions that didn't go smoothly, or other impactful events that caused you distress but were not necessarily a direct threat to your life or integrity.

If you have experienced one or more of these events, your brain would have stored all those little-T experiences in the "never to be repeated" basket and sound the anxiety alarms with present situations that feel even remotely similar. Let's look at some examples of how little-T trauma can trigger anxiety.

You may or may not be aware that nausea is one of the most common symptoms of anxiety, and many of my clients have struggled in some way or another with symptoms of nausea, vomiting, and diarrhea, resulting in more anxiety. In Vivian's case, it had to do with a little-T trauma that she had completely forgotten about.

Vivian started therapeutic coaching for anxiety when she found herself avoiding going out into public. She felt anxious about being in public and didn't understand why. The more she avoided going out, the more anxious she became.

As we worked through the Empower step, Vivian began to uncover her what if questions and the fears she had about needing a bathroom while in public and not being able to find one. As we explored these concerns in more depth, Vivian also realized the only reason she might feel nauseous or suddenly need a bathroom was if she suddenly became anxious while she was out. Vivian was terrified of becoming anxious and nauseous in public. A clear example of anxiety about anxiety.

A deeper dive into Vivian's why me story revealed an experience when she was seven years old and had become unwell while visiting her uncle. Her nausea was quite sudden and she was unable to reach the bathroom before vomiting in her uncle's house. She felt a deep sense of embarrassment which was made even worse when Vivian's uncle became angry about the mess he had to clean up. Her seven-year-old brain figured that being sick and causing a mess threatened her belonging and acceptance (and thus her survival).

As time went by, Vivian continued to have anxious thoughts about feeling nauseous or vomiting. She worried about having to clean up the mess if it happened and the guilt she might feel if someone else had to assist her while she was sick. Vivian's primary symptom of anxiety also happened to be nausea so her concerns and worried thoughts would then turn into nausea, which would perpetuate the worries and anxiety, creating a self-perpetuating downward spiral. Despite these worries, Vivian had never had another experience of uncontrolled vomiting. Her fears were based solely on that one experience she had as a child.

Another example of a trauma triggering anxiety and, potentially, stuck anxiety is the experience of a panic attack. Most people agree that the experience of a panic attack is a traumatic experience. The symptoms of a panic attack can make you think that you are dying, which leaves many people feeling incapacitated and out of control. Naturally, your brain puts this experience in the "never to be repeated" basket.

While in most cases it is the trauma of the panic attack that triggers ongoing anxiety, in some cases it is a little more complicated. Kelly joined a group program with me because she was struggling with health anxiety. But Kelly couldn't figure out why she was struggling with this degree of concern over her health and described herself as a previously outgoing, carefree person who had never been aware of any anxiety symptoms. She had come to a point where she scrutinized and feared every single creak and groan her body made. She felt concerned about a twitch in her eye, a ringing in her ear, a pain in her throat. Everything felt sinister, and she worried about every new symptom or sensation she experienced. The more she worried about her physical symptoms, the more anxiety she experienced and the more physical symptoms she experienced. Classic stuck anxiety.

As we explored Kelly's situation during the first step of the E.A.S.E. Method, she explained that she had become unwell with COVID-19 a few months prior. In the midst of the illness, Kelly had struggled with respiratory problems and couldn't catch her breath. It felt frightening, and it seemed to be a symptom that never lifted, even after she recovered from COVID-19. Kelly continued to struggle with shortness of breath, which, naturally, concerned her. And the more concerned she became, the more she struggled with the shortness of breath. Her worries kept escalating until she was worried about her health in general. She began frequently checking in on her physical symptoms and ever-increasing anxiety.

As we discussed Kelly's experience of COVID-19, she described feeling tired and one day where she struggled to catch her breath. She also experienced a racing heart at the time and a firm belief that she was, in fact, dying that day. She had felt very anxious, and while she did not recognize it at the time, it is likely that Kelly experienced a panic attack that day.

Not only was the experience of COVID-19 unpleasant, but the experience of a panic attack complicated things for her brain, which associated the shortness of breath with a threat to her survival. Kelly's belief in her ability to bounce back and heal was challenged by this experience, and her amygdala started screaming for her to pay attention to her shortness of breath. This is a clear cycle of anxiety about anxiety, as the shortness of breath was a symptom of the anxiety but also the trigger for the anxiety.

While I can share many more examples of trauma triggering anxiety, there are also many people for whom anxiety has other root causes. This leads us to the third common reason for anxiety: to get you to pay attention to something you are avoiding.

When You're Avoiding Something

The role of anxiety is to get you to pay attention. And often, we find ourselves in situations that do not serve us, but we keep on going for whatever reason. Perhaps this is an unhealthy relationship that you're afraid to leave or a job that does not align with your values. Maybe you need to make a big decision that feels difficult or have an uncomfortable conversation with someone, but you would prefer to avoid the confrontation because potential conflict feels uncomfortable or scary. Intuitively, you always know what is in your best interest. However, sometimes your core beliefs and society's expectations can get in the way and leave you feeling like you don't have a choice to leave the situation even when you do.

Perhaps you believe you should be grateful for what you have and, thus, decide to stay in the job that makes you unhappy. Your intuition is telling you you're not happy but the belief that you should feel grateful for a secure job gets in the way. Or maybe you feel the weight of expectation for you to make your relationship work, despite it being unhealthy. Sometimes, our beliefs that our needs are too much or too demanding stop us from having the assertive conversations we need to have.

No matter what the situation is, when you are behaving in a way that goes against what you intuitively know to be right for you, your anxiety will flare up to let you know that you need to pay attention.

Chantelle had been married for twelve years to her high school sweetheart. Their relationship had been described as a match made in heaven, and her partner had supported her through some of the most difficult times of her life as she worked on healing significant childhood traumas. He had stood by her and helped her through difficult issues around trust and intimacy. By the time she came to see me, in her early thirties, Chantelle was functioning well as she pursued further studies and built her career. She experienced her partner as needy and felt as if the relationship had changed somehow. It was clear that neither she nor her partner felt fulfilled anymore, and she kept thinking that he might be holding her back somehow.

However, she felt like it wasn't acceptable to even entertain thoughts about breaking up. How could she break a match made in heaven? After all, he had stood by her in her most difficult times. Surely, she owed it to him to stay in the relationship and make it work. So, Chantelle pushed thoughts of dissatisfaction with her marriage out of her mind and continued to throw herself into her work.

The more she avoided thoughts about her discontent in the relationship, the more anxiety she felt. She couldn't understand why she felt so anxious when everything was going smoothly. She was focusing on her career, enjoying her friendships, and exercising. At home, her relationship with her husband became more detached, and while they still loved each other and were getting along, there seemed to be something missing for them both. Neither was prepared to think about separation.

The anxiety continued until Chantelle decided to explore the reasons for anxiety and face what it was saying. She wasn't happy in her relationship anymore, and if she was honest, neither was her husband. They had outgrown each other, and in many ways, they were standing in the way of each other's personal growth and development. They didn't have children and, other than an expectation to stay together, there was no other reason to force the relationship to work. But Chantelle didn't feel she had the right to end the relationship after everything her husband had done for her. Her beliefs about what was expected of her flew in the face of what she knew to be necessary for both herself and her husband: They had outgrown one another and she believed it was time to go their separate ways.

Chantelle faced her truth and communicated this to her husband. Despite difficult and uncomfortable conversations, her anxiety lessened and eventually disappeared completely. They gave couples counselling a try and eventually decided to go their separate ways. This story does not suggest that marriages should end at a whim. In fact, there are many options to explore when you realize you are unhappy in your relationship. This story illustrates that, at some point in life, we all face very difficult decisions that do not always have an ideal outcome. And the decision to face what you have been avoiding is rarely an easy one. If it were easy, you would have done it already. These decisions are often accompanied by uncomfortable changes and unknown outcomes. In the interest of remaining safe and comfortable, you choose to avoid making the change or facing the uncertainty. But intuitively, you know the current status quo does not serve you and change is inevitable.

Anxiety is the brain's way of getting you to pay attention. The current situation, which does not serve you, also does not aid your survival. In fact, remaining in such a space may very well threaten your wellbeing, which is why anxiety rings its primitive alarm.

When Your System Is Stressed

The final most common reason for anxiety is a stressed system. And by system, I am referring to your physical, mental, emotional, or spiritual state. In this sense, we understand your system holistically, and when any part of your system becomes stressed, you may feel anxiety. Burnout, for example, is a common problem nowadays. A side effect of burnout is often anxiety. Many people become stressed and anxious, feeling exhausted and unable to cope with their work or life challenges.

Stress is an interesting thing. And it has a lot to do with how we perceive the situation. When life or work feels challenging and we feel like we have the resources to meet the challenge, we will feel mentally stimulated. But we need to have the resources to meet the sorts of challenges we face in daily life. If we have enough money, time, energy, or support, the challenges feel good and we may even feel energized and motivated by this level of challenge. Some call this a state of flow, and it keeps us feeling like we are making progress in life.

Sometimes these challenges can push us into a zone when we no longer feel like we have the resources (time, money, energy, or emotional strength) to meet them. We begin to feel exhausted and stretched thin. It can begin to feel unsafe when we don't feel like we have what it takes to meet the challenge presented to us and we may move into a fight or flight response. Many people refer to this as "burnout." And it is often where anxiety rears its head.

Burnout and Mental Stress

Angela was the head of a primary school and needed to take time off work when she began struggling with severe anxiety that kept her up at night, resulting in nausea, dizziness, and poor vision. Her anxiety had become so stuck that she was unable to physically function on the job so she decided to take a few days off work. As she spent time at home and explored her situation in our coaching sessions, she began to realize that her work demands had far surpassed her perceived resources.

As a wife and mother of two, Angela would return home as late as 7 or 8 pm from work. This left her very little time to do household chores or spend quality time with her family. She felt the demands of work piling high and then experienced guilt at not managing to get through it all in one day. She would stay late to ensure her to-do list was completed before heading home. Her belief was that if she didn't get everything done today she would have to do even more tomorrow. She felt too guilty to delegate more of the work to her colleagues because they were stretched thin too.

After months of facing these increasing work challenges and then needing to take care of her sick father, Angela finally buckled under the weight and experienced what most would call burnout. When the challenges you face exceed your mental, emotional, and situational resources to cope, you may begin to feel so overwhelmed with anxiety that you can't function. She struggled to sleep, experienced nausea, and suffered from persistent anxiety. Angela felt on edge all day long, struggled to concentrate, and felt like she could no longer handle her emotions well. She would have been forced to take more time off from work had it not been for the blessing of the summer holidays ahead.

Anxiety knows when you are in over your head. Your amygdala can sense the threat to your survival in the perceived lack of resources and the mounting challenges, and it begins to scream at you to slow down, take care of yourself, and avoid the impending fall. People rarely heed the call of anxiety at this point. They believe they have no choice but to soldier on with their mounting challenges and escalating levels of stress. They have an extra glass of wine to relax at night, try some medication to help them feel better, and just continue along the same path.

Anxiety wants to keep you safe. When you stop to listen to what it is telling you, you'll be better equipped to change course, take better care of yourself, and avoid burnout. Burnout happens when you have pushed yourself too hard without providing enough self-nurturing or self-care. It is like driving your car for years on end and never servicing it. Eventually, the problems will mount, and the engine will need to be repaired.

Emotional and Spiritual Stress

Emotional distress can trigger anxiety too. Situations that feel uncomfortable or emotionally taxing and leave you in a vulnerable state often lead to anxiety. Perhaps you have lost someone close to you or you find yourself in a relationship that is less than ideal. Maybe life has handed you lemon after lemon, and you have lost the recipe for lemonade. On a daily basis, it feels as if your heart is broken; loneliness and sadness have become familiar feelings to you. After a while, you might notice anxiety creeping in there too.

Anxiety only wants you to pay attention. Sadness and loneliness are not our natural way of being. They indicate that some of our core emotional needs are not being met. And when they continue long enough, anxiety is going to pop up as an alarm to say that our system isn't doing well and needs some attention.

There isn't always something you can do about loss or tragedy in life, but sometimes there is. Perhaps you need more support but haven't asked for help. Maybe you need to engage in self-care or look at your inner self-talk. Whatever the case may be, the anxiety is asking you to pay attention because the ongoing emotional distress is indicating that something needs to be changed.

While mental and emotional stress are far more common, spiritual stress can also lead to heightened anxiety. Some people enter a spiritual crisis when their worldview and perceptions have been shaken. Maybe they've decided to leave their religion, convert to a different one, or begin searching for a deeper sense of spirituality and meaning in their life. They find themselves struggling to adjust to their new beliefs or opinions, and their anxiety is sounding the alarm that all is not well.

Spiritual beliefs bring a sense of safety and certainty. When they are rocked, it can cause anxiety as that safety is challenged. In African cultures, for example, some people might experience anxiety and a host of other ailments when not heeding the call to become a traditional healer. In other religions and beliefs anxiety is a sign they are not following their path. While this may reflect misaligned values that need to be addressed, the anxiety is there to get them to pay attention. In every situation, anxiety serves a purpose.

Physical Stress

Physical stress can also trigger anxiety. We know that not enough rest and lack of nutrition from a poor diet can both contribute to physical stress and poor health. We also know that lack of vitamins and minerals and hormone imbalances can create physical stress. And we know these physical stress responses can be associated with anxiety. I always recommend that you have a thorough physical checkup with your health provider to rule out possible deficiencies and imbalances that may be contributing to, or worsening, your anxiety.

Many studies have shown that a deficiency in magnesium is linked to heightened states of anxiety. A robust review of these studies conducted in 2012 supported the emerging evidence that reduced levels of magnesium are associated with anxiety.[10] A more recent article published in the National Library of Medicine suggested that "Vitamin B$_{12}$ deficiency can have distressing neuropsychiatric symptoms" and play a causative role in mental health difficulties such as anxiety, depression, and psychosis.[11] Health professionals have also asserted that lower levels of Vitamin D are associated with increased anxiety, which is confirmed by multiple studies.[12] We also know that hormone changes can affect anxiety and many women entering perimenopause experience surges of anxiety, if not persistently escalated levels of anxiety.[13]

If we understand the body as a holistic system requiring the right nutrients to maintain optimal functioning, then it makes sense that any deficiency or surplus could result in an imbalance in the body and put the system under stress. This means that the body isn't functioning as it should. Things aren't right.

Due to the perpetual separation of mind and body in the medical world, we have a limited (yet growing) understanding of how one affects the other. An imbalance in the body can result in a negative effect on the mental state, and vice versa. When your body is under stress, that is likely to affect your brain and mental functioning, and often anxiety pops up to alert you to a threat to your physical wellness.

Answering the "Why Now" Question

I share these deeper explorations of the reasons for anxiety to help you answer the important "why now?" question. Not only does this increase your understanding of the anxiety you experience and help you gain back some control, but it also provides you with the opportunity to use anxiety as it was intended: to keep you safe. These four main reasons for anxiety provide you with a basis from which you can continue to empower yourself by listening to your anxiety and using its wisdom in your life. When you understand that anxiety is acting in your best interest, you can truly begin to see it as an ally. This is how you can begin to use anxiety for personal growth.

Time To Take Action:

Once you have interrupted the cycle of anxiety about anxiety, you can begin to lean in and listen to what anxiety was asking you to pay attention to in the first place. Here are some self-reflective questions to help you discover the messages anxiety has for you. If you are using a journal then use these questions as journal prompts:

- Consider the core beliefs you have explored in a previous exercise. What current situations or circumstances could trigger these core beliefs?
- What areas of your life feel out of your control to change? Are there difficult or uncomfortable situations, relationships, or decisions you have been avoiding? What fears or concerns stop you from addressing these areas? Are there core beliefs or past traumas that stop you from addressing these areas?
- Take a good look at your physical, mental, emotional, and spiritual system. Are there areas that need some TLC and care? What physical, mental, emotional, or spiritual needs are not being met by yourself or by others and what can you do to meet these?

CHAPTER THIRTEEN

Using Anxiety for Personal Growth

As you get better at listening to your anxiety and identifying the reasons for it, you will begin to grow and learn in ways that were never available to you when you were so busy resisting anxiety and fighting with it. You're beginning to see that our "negative" emotional responses are a signal to us that something is amiss. Feeling happy, content, and fulfilled indicates that things are going well. Anxiety and your other uncomfortable emotions can become fantastic guides for you in all areas of your life. These emotions are a sign of mental health, not illness. Your emotions are guides that help you get your needs met so you can live a safe, fulfilling, and meaningful life.

To demonstrate, let's go back to Nora who was anxious and miserable with her work-from-home situation. What did she learn from her anxiety? Understanding that she felt isolated and needed to work on her core beliefs and unrelenting standards, Nora decided to move her home office to a coworking space and embark on some deeper inner critic work. She began to soften the high expectations she had of herself and the critical self-talk she often engaged in. She allowed herself more flexibility, and therefore more enjoyment, in her workday. Where previously she wouldn't allow herself to meet up with a friend for coffee in the middle of the day, she started to relax her stringent standards for herself and was able to lean in to the advantage of fully flexible working hours.

Nora also took a careful look at her financial needs—something she had been avoiding due to anxiety—and made changes to her budget that took some of the pressure off her need to earn a certain amount per month. This reduced her fear of not earning enough. Because of these changes, she no longer felt that overwhelming sense of dread each morning.

If Nora had decided to continue trying to get rid of the anxiety, she would not have had the opportunity to make these positive changes to her beliefs and actions.

Using Core Beliefs for Personal Growth

When core beliefs have triggered anxiety, it presents a clear opportunity to work with the false core belief causing the problem. Remember, all negative core beliefs are untrue and can keep you stuck in old ways of thinking and behaving that are not serving you. Rationally, you know it is not true that you need to be perfect to be valued. You logically understand that you are not too much or too demanding and that your needs are important. Even those beliefs created around earlier little-T events, such as being bullied or laughed at, are not true. When anxiety rings alarm bells because those core beliefs and experiences have been triggered, it normally does so from an inner child perspective. The trigger stems from the place of the child that you once were who had those experiences and created those beliefs. Now, those beliefs stand in the way of your ability to get the results you want in life.

In other words, the beliefs belong to a little child who faced the situations that created them. This means that the present-day accuracy of these beliefs really is questionable given the fact that you are no longer a child. The world has changed, but your beliefs, and consequent actions may be stuck in the past. As an adult, you have more knowledge, resources, and understanding and your basic survival no longer depends on caregivers accepting and loving you.

You are not the same child that answered that math question wrong in fifth grade. You are a capable adult. You are not the same child who was told to be seen and not heard. You are an adult now and you make your own decisions. You are not the child who depended on their parents to love and approve of them. You are an adult and your survival no longer depends on getting love and approval. It is time to let go of those old beliefs.

Seeing anxiety as an ally means that anxiety can alert you to those specific areas of personal growth that need your attention. My husband, for example, was eventually able to identify his core belief and work on his expectation of being a failure. As he did so, he opened himself up to new possibilities. Letting go of his Failure schema, we have enjoyed raising a second child, immigrated to a new country, moved from one side of the country to another, and he has started another business. Had he not done this work, he would have continued to limit himself and his potential by continuing to buy into the core belief that he would inevitably fail.

Kath identified the belief that her feelings were intolerable to herself and unacceptable to others. It meant that she stayed guarded in her relationships, sharing only small pieces of herself with others. It also meant that she restricted where she went and how she behaved. Since challenging that core belief, Kath has allowed herself to show vulnerability, be more assertive and get back to enjoying the adventures her life has to offer despite not always being perfectly put together.

While many people think anxiety is what's holding them back from growing or moving forward, it often ends up being the key to figuring out how to grow and what to do differently so that you can get your needs met.

Nora's exploration of her core beliefs helped her see how she could make valuable and positive changes to her daily work routine, which left her feeling more relaxed and fulfilled. And Angela was able to identify that her work demanded far more time and energy than she actually had. She began making significant changes and putting firmer boundaries around her work hours. Angela realized she had been neglecting her real needs for self-care so she began prioritizing walks in the afternoon, which doubled up as quality time spent with her kids and husband. Had she not listened to the call of anxiety, she would have continued down a path of stressful self-destruction and distancing herself from her family by working too much.

The call from anxiety is to get you to pay attention. What is the core belief that is standing in the way of your true potential? When you make room for anxiety and listen to it you can use it as an ally to alert you to areas of your life that may not be serving you.

Understanding Little-T Traumas for Personal Growth

Anxiety may alert you to the little-T traumas that have contributed to your anxiety. Instead of feeling frozen in that morning meeting, stammering and unsure of what to say, you might be more aware of the 5th grade version of you that is afraid to put yourself out there and risk social rejection. Knowing that you are no longer that little child and that you have more resources and charisma than you had back then, you might now be able to face those old demons.

Awareness can help you turn your reactions into responses. When anxiety pops up we tend to react. We might feel the need to escape, or we might freeze in fear. In many cases we don't understand why we react the way we do. All that confusion and anxiety can lead to avoiding those situations, which ends up limiting ourselves and our personal growth. No more morning meetings if I am going to freak out in anxiety, right? But when you understand that the alarm was ringing because of a time gone by when this same experience felt threatening, you can choose to respond differently. You can now employ your adult understanding of the situation to calm your anxiety and choose a response that helps you get your needs met.

In this way Vivian was able to process the little-T trauma of becoming unwell at her uncle's house and recognize that she was now better equipped to deal with an event of nausea (even if in public). Before this awareness she simply reacted to the idea of spontaneous public outings (where she worried she would become nauseous) with anxiety and avoidance. With her new awareness of the little-T trauma, she was able to stop the vicious cycle of anxiety about anxiety, which meant she was able to plan Saturday morning outings with her son and her partner. Had Vivian not been prepared to delve into her anxiety, she would have continued avoiding spontaneous outings and missed out on quality time with her family.

Ending Avoidance for Personal Growth

You're starting to see it clearly now, right? That anxiety is merely an alarm system designed to get you to pay attention. And we have explored the various ways that avoiding paying attention only makes the alarm sound louder. When you learn to lean in and listen you are challenged to pay attention to the issues in your life you may be avoiding.

What big decision have you put on the back burner because it feels too difficult to make? What relationship is not working for you but you're too afraid to address the reality of what it means to face this? What needs are not being met in your own life that you are sacrificing in the interest of others?

These may feel like uncomfortable topics but they can often lead to important discussions that help you grow and get your needs met. Addressing them is often the only way forward (and you may find anxiety reducing significantly as you Engage in this new way).

You have to be both vulnerable and brave to listen to your anxiety and act on its wisdom. You are developing the ability to make room for your feelings and recognizing that those feelings always concern one important factor: Whether your needs are being met or not.

As you take your newfound alliance with anxiety a little further you may consider what physical, emotional, mental, or spiritual changes are required for you to get back to living a life you truly love and feel proud of.

Time To Take Action

Using Core Beliefs For Personal Growth Exercise

Now that anxiety has alerted you to the potential core beliefs that are operating in your life, it is time to challenge them and move toward more positive and rational beliefs that can serve you.

Use the following as self-reflective questions or journal prompts to help you:

- Consider the core beliefs you identified in chapter 2. In what way do these core beliefs get in the way of you having your needs for love, validation, connection, safety, fun, and independence met?
- These core beliefs were formed when you were much younger. Consider yourself as an adult now and explore how your situation is different from when you were younger. How do these core beliefs still apply or not apply to your life as an adult?
- Can you find evidence in your life that disproves the beliefs you hold about yourself? Are there instances in which they are not true?
- What would be more appropriate beliefs to hold about yourself as an adult now? Consider what you believe about other people close to you and how you might apply those same beliefs to your own situation.

Understanding Past Trauma For Personal Growth Exercise

- Anxiety can alert you to past traumas that need processing. Are there past experiences that need to be explored and discussed with a therapist to help you process them?
- Anxiety can alert you to the areas of your life that require attention. What areas require you to take action now? Write a list of important situations, relationships, and decisions that need your attention now or in the near future.

CHAPTER FOURTEEN

Self-Reflection to Help You Listen to Anxiety

Understanding the reasons for anxiety is usually enough to pique the interest of most clients. Once they understand there is a deeper function of anxiety and it would help them grow if they were willing to listen, they are usually keen on knowing what they can do to open that door and hear what their anxiety has to say.

It always starts with a willingness to truly listen. As with all conversations, you need to be present and open to hearing what the other is saying. Remember the last time you tried having a conversation with your partner or adolescent child and they continued looking at their phone? Do you recall how you felt trying to get their attention when they were clearly distracted by social media? I am willing to bet you lost enthusiasm for what you were saying and may very well have given up.

Successful conversations require two people actively participating. At any given moment, one should be actively talking and the other actively listening. In the conversation with anxiety, you are the listener. And that means you must actively listen, stay present, and give your anxiety space to just exist and be even when it feels uncomfortable for you.

Anxiety cannot speak with words so you need to become more familiar with it as you learn to understand the different ways it communicates with you. The more you lean in to your anxiety and allow it to exist, the better acquainted you will become with it and the more you will fine-tune your understanding of how and why it shows up.

Always remember that you are the expert on you. You really do have the answer when you explore the reasons for your anxiety or contemplate the self-reflective questions offered inside this book. As you ask yourself the question you may feel or hear the answer as an inner knowing. I find it helps to journal and write down the thoughts that pop up for me. Many people question the validity of their inner voice or think the answer they've come up with is too simple. They doubt themselves and their inner knowing. Please give yourself permission to be the expert on yourself. If an answer pops up when you ask yourself a question, allow that to be true and explore it a little further. You don't have to act on it right away, but you don't have to push it away or immediately devalue it either.

The process of leaning in and listening requires patience and a willingness to get to know yourself a little more. It may feel confusing and strange when you first get started. Let's explore three more ways in which you can learn to lean in and be with anxiety to help you along.

Anxiety Body Scan

The first exercise is a mindfulness-based body scan, which will allow you to become more familiar with anxiety and how it shows up in your body. As you engage with this practice, try to focus on your ability to explore with curiosity. Remain accepting of what you find rather than slipping into a mindset of rejecting it or creating anxiety about the anxiety you are experiencing.

The goal is to become better acquainted with your anxiety and learn more about how it talks to you. This gentle exercise will also allow you to practice the art of observing your experiences without becoming too attached to them or creating more thoughts and feelings about them.

You can read through the below script first and then close your eyes and run through it on your own. Or feel

free to download the audio version from the website
www.theunstuckinitiative.com/giftofanxiety

1. Make yourself comfortable in a seated or lying down position. Adjust your level of comfort until you find yourself able to relax without holding tension in your neck, shoulders, or legs.

2. Allow your eyes to gently close or keep them open and gaze forward without focusing on anything in particular.

3. Take a gentle breath in and then gently expel the air. Allow this to happen naturally. Do not force yourself to breath particularly slowly or deeply—simply allow the breath to come and go.

4. Notice your lungs filling, your chest rising, and then the fall of the chest as the air is released.

5. Now take a moment to notice the space between your inhales and exhales.

6. As you notice what is happening in your body, allow yourself to enter a space of gentle exploration. Simply observe what is happening in your body without any judgment or feelings about what you find.

7. Continue to breathe calmly and gently as you focus your attention on your feet and your legs. Explore both feet and both legs with your mind. Notice how your feet touch the floor or the surface you are lying on. Observe their position. Explore any sensations in your feet.

8. Next, allow your awareness to travel up your legs. Observe what is there. Notice the sensation of clothing on your legs, the position your legs are in, and any other sensations you might find.

9. Do not label any of the sensations other than to simply observe with curiosity. They are neither good nor bad. They simply are.

10. Now allow your awareness to travel into your lower abdomen, hips, and low back as you explore these areas. Notice the contact your body makes with the surface you

are sitting on or lying down on. Notice your clothing as it touches your skin and observe any other sensations you might have in this area. Breathe and relax.

11. Bring awareness up into your stomach and chest area. Notice what is happening there. Observe any tightness or tension. Explore any signs of anxiety you might feel. Simply observe how things are.

12. Do not allow your brain to get tangled up in thoughts about good and bad. Keep your awareness in a curious and accepting state. You are safe, and the anxiety simply is what it is. Notice where you feel it, if at all, in your tummy and chest area.

13. Observe any changes that occur as you become aware of those sensations. If they shift into something different, follow them with acceptance and simply observe. Again, do not label or judge the experience as anything other than what it is.

14. When you feel you have observed everything there is to notice in your stomach and chest area, bring your awareness into your back and shoulders. Again, notice your position, any tension, and the way your clothes touch your skin. Observe any sensations of tightness or anxiety there. Simply observe how it is in your back and shoulders. Allow it to be as it is.

15. Next, bring awareness into your neck and head. Become aware of the muscles in your neck and the sensations you may experience there. What does it feel like in your neck?

16. Then move into your head and scalp. Observe the sensations on your head around your scalp and in your face. Notice but do not label. Suspend judgment and continue to practice gentle, curious exploration.

17. Now become aware of your eyes, cheeks, jaw, and lips. Become aware of your tongue inside your mouth. Notice what is there. Observe any sensations, tension, pulling, or clenching. Simply observe. You do not need to change anything. It all is exactly as it is, and trying to change

it implies that you have judged it to be wrong. It isn't wrong. It simply is.

18. Now bring your awareness to your emotions. What are you feeling in this moment? What can you notice about the thoughts that attach to those feelings?

19. If you notice anxiety as an emotional experience, what does that feel like and where in your body does it show up the most? Simply allow it to be there. It is what it is, and you are safe as you continue your gentle exploration of this inner world.

20. As you explore any anxious sensations, or perhaps other feelings that have shown up, notice what thoughts are attached to the anxiety. Where does your mind naturally pull you as you feel into the anxiety? Do not allow yourself to be swept away with these thoughts. Simply observe the thought and let it go.

21. It might help to say "Oh, there I am thinking about..." and then let that thought go as you return your awareness to your body. Don't beat yourself up if you get distracted. Just notice it and return your attention to your body without judgement.

22. Become aware of the body just as it is now. Notice the entire body now and all the sensations. Observe the sensations as they occur. Continue to suspend your judgment or evaluation of how your body feels and continue to practice simple acceptance of what is. It is what it is.

23. Now become aware of your body in the room you are in. Stretch your awareness into the space you take up in this world and the area that surrounds you. Notice what you can feel and hear around you. No need to open your eyes; simply sense the temperature of the air, the sounds you might hear, and the feeling of the room around you.

24. And when you are ready, open your eyes, and come back to your regular awareness.

The anxiety body scan is a great way to get present and feel the sensations of anxiety. As you practice more often, you may become more aware of thoughts attached to the anxiety. Perhaps there are particular worries that come up with the anxiety. Maybe you find yourself thinking back to a particular event in the past. The thoughts that pop up are often a clue to what the anxiety is trying to get you to pay attention to. In these moments of stillness and willingness to explore, the anxiety has a chance to get you to see what it's talking about. These worries may be around an issue you are avoiding or a core belief that has been triggered. Past events or memories that bubble up could indicate a past trauma that has been triggered, leaving you feeling unsafe in the present.

Creating the space to be with and listen to anxiety offers you an opportunity to learn from yourself. Remember to trust yourself and allow those answers to come. Being open gives you a chance to see why anxiety is there and what it wants you to pay attention to.

Mindfulness of Emotions

You can use the following practice on any emotional state—it is not limited to anxiety. Practicing mindfulness of your emotions allows you to be with your emotional experience without attaching any further emotions to it. Remember how acknowledgment and permission help emotional states to process and flow? Practicing mindfulness with your emotions is a powerful way to allow this to happen.

Follow these steps when you notice a strong feeling or anxiety coming up:

1. Take a gentle, deep breath in and expand your chest and belly. Do this with the intention of creating space for both you and the emotion you are experiencing.

2. Now fully observe and notice the feeling. Can you name it? Recognizing the feeling is the first step in fully acknowledging it and allowing it. It could be anxiety or nervousness. Perhaps it is fear or irritability. Become aware of the feeling you are experiencing and name it.

3. Accept this emotion. It is a real and valid feeling and it cannot harm you. Remind yourself of the impermanence of emotional states and recognize that this will subside, so it is okay to let it in temporarily as you observe it.

4. Simply observe and accept the feeling. If judgmental thoughts come to your mind like *I have nothing to feel anxious about, Why won't this go away?* and *I shouldn't be feeling this way right now,* just observe them and let those thoughts pass. These are judgments that do not allow acceptance of the current state.

5. Explore the feeling. Where do you feel it most in your body? What do you notice about your posture when you have this feeling? What is your facial expression as you have this feeling? Where else do you notice it? Do you notice sensations in your hands, jaw, neck, shoulders, or other areas of your body?

6. Explore what else comes with this feeling. One emotional response is often a cover for another. Anger often comes before sadness. Irritability often comes before anxiety. It is not always so, but it could be. Observe what else is there with the original feeling.

7. Now, allow thoughts to come and pass. Imagine you are looking at the thought and then flicking it away, into the air, in order to pick up another thought and observe it. Notice any thoughts that come up with this feeling. Do not hold onto any one thought for too long; simply flick it away and allow the next one into your awareness.

8. Lastly, recognize that you are not defined by the feelings or thoughts you have observed. These are simply your experience, but they do not define you. You are not anxious, you experience anxiety. You are not angry, you experience

anger. You are not worried, you experience worry. Remind yourself of this as you close the practice.

Self-Reflection Journal Prompts

At the center of your being, you have the answer; You know who you are and you know what you want. —Lao Tzu

Self-reflection tools are powerful therapeutic strategies to get you to slow down and pay attention to your own thoughts and feelings. We are usually so busy racing from one activity to another that we rarely take the time to simply pause and notice what we are feeling, let alone thinking. Much of our lives are lived on autopilot. But taking a moment to look inward and listen to our inner wisdom can be revealing.

All we need to do is take the time and ask the right questions. It might feel really nice to treat yourself to a brand new, beautiful notebook and pen. But be prepared to be raw, messy, and imperfect within the white crisp pages. Journaling is about being honest, not about being well presented. So here is your invitation to use the journal prompts below to be beautifully raw and messy within the pages of your journal. If you do not enjoy journalling, then I invite you to use these prompts as self-reflective questions to explore in meditation or times of stillness.

- Reflect on one of the greatest life lessons you have learned. What happened and what did you learn about yourself? How can you draw on the wisdom from that lesson now?
- With an open heart and listening intently to that inner child inside of you, what do they most need right now?
- What can you do or change in your life right now to be able to focus more on your own wellbeing?
- If you could change one thing right now, what would it be and why? Or perhaps you wouldn't change anything right now, why not?

- What values do you hold to be most important in your life and relationships? List as many as come to you. Now, looking at that list, how many of these values might be missing from your life? Take some time to reflect on why that is and what you could do more or less of to increase the presence of your most important values. Remember, this is not an opportunity to beat yourself up about what might be missing. This is a self-compassionate exercise to help you get realigned with your important values.
- Take a deep breath and step into your anxiety. Try to imagine you are the anxiety. Now write a letter to yourself from your anxiety. What are you afraid of or worried about? What do you need most?
- When you are ready, write back to your anxiety from yourself. What assurances can you offer? What changes will you be making?

CHAPTER FIFTEEN

From Anxiety about Anxiety
to Trauma Resolution

Melanie, an active woman with a healthy social life and budding career, joined me for a group program because, despite her best efforts, she continued to struggle with debilitating anxiety before events. Whether it was a major event like a wedding or work presentation or something smaller, such as a gathering of friends or even a date night with her partner, Melanie would feel anxious beforehand. She would often start to feel anxious hours ahead of time because she worried she would feel anxious at the event. Melanie had created a routine of using the bathroom for a few hours the morning of any event to get control of her anxiety symptoms, which largely consisted of what she called "tummy troubles."

If the wedding was out of town, Melanie would need to plan weeks in advance to ensure that the hotel she would be staying in had an adequate bathroom for her to use. She worried when staying at her boyfriend's house because the bathroom was close to the bedroom and she wanted to have privacy. And she would experience heightened anxiety prior to the event if she was staying anywhere where she would need to share a bathroom with more than just her partner because she didn't want to be rushed when using the bathroom. The worry and preparation that surrounded needing a bathroom prior to an event caused exhaustion and despair for Melanie. She couldn't enjoy the planning or preparing for any event because she was always riddled with concerns and what if questions.

As Melanie started the first step (Empower) of the E.A.S.E.

Method and explored some of the what if questions and beliefs keeping her anxiety stuck, she began to realize that her real fear was about becoming anxious at the event and not being able to find a toilet. Like Vivian, Melanie was worried that her anxiety would get the better of her while she was out and about, leaving her nauseous and helpless.

This is a very common symptom and fear with anxiety. Instead of avoiding the events altogether as Vivian had done, Melanie tried to control the anxiety by attending to tummy troubles in advance and spending hours in the bathroom beforehand. This is a classic case of responding to anxiety with Nervous Control.

Instead of accepting her anxiety, she was fearfully and meticulously planning and trying to control anxiety with ample bathroom time before the event. Melanie was experiencing anxiety about anxiety. Her need to control anxiety also created more anxiety about whether the bathroom conditions would be suitable, which was a result of her Nervous Control response toward anxiety.

Melanie felt stuck. While she recognized the importance of being able to accept anxiety and let it subside, an important piece was missing for her. She simply could not understand why she would feel so anxious about needing a toilet at an event and not finding one. She could not remember a time in her adult life when this had, in fact, occurred. And she had attended many events.

During an individual session, a deeper dive into Melanie's story revealed an important experience at around the age of six. Melanie recalled attending a family gathering when she experienced a sudden—and violent—case of food poisoning. While in the throes of non-stop vomiting, Melanie struggled to take a breath and began to panic. As a result, she experienced a panic attack amid the violent retching. Her mother, naturally worried, rang the ambulance, as she was concerned for her daughter's wellbeing. This meant that Melanie's food poisoning and becoming suddenly unwell had completely disrupted the family gathering, leaving her feeling embarrassed and ashamed.

Remember that panic attacks in and of themselves can be traumatic experiences. At the time of a panic attack, the brain can start to believe you might be dying. When you struggle to breathe or feel chest pain, you may think you are having a heart attack and that fear that you might die can feel overwhelming and traumatizing. While a six-year-old child cannot comprehend that they are having a panic attack, their brain is certainly aware of the struggle to breathe and fears that their survival is immediately threatened. Consequently, the experience of panic itself becomes a "never to be repeated" experience as far as the amygdala is concerned.

In Melanie's case, however, the panic attack itself was not the trauma. Melanie was not afraid of panic attacks. The feeling of not being able to breathe and vomiting was the traumatic experience. Her brain had connected this panic attack and not breathing with the nausea and vomiting. As a result, becoming nauseous and sick had been stored by her brain as a traumatic event never to be repeated.

Remember that when current situations feel or seem like past events, the amygdala might ring the alarm bells to get you to pay attention. This is exactly what Melanie's brain was doing. As she neared a big event with a gathering of people, her amygdala would sound the alarms in the hopes of creating awareness about the potential dangers associated with becoming sick at events. After all, that childhood experience felt like a near-death one.

This trauma created low-level anxiety before an event which created the associated symptoms of nausea and tummy troubles that then served to fuel and exacerbate the anxiety. The amygdala was left screaming, *You see! You're getting sick! This must not happen at the event!* In her desperate attempt to control the anxiety and establish some sense of safety, Melanie automatically turned to alleviating tummy troubles before they could affect her at an event.

As Melanie uncovered this traumatic experience and linked it to her persistent anxiety around events, she felt more able to let go of the need to control the anxiety beforehand. She was able to talk her poor amygdala down and reassure herself that, as an adult, she was better able to manage such incidents should they occur. Melanie understood the need to stop the cycle of Nervous Control and lean in to experiencing some of the anxiety. And as she did this, she noticed the anxiety begin to subside. By the end of the program, Melanie was able to present in front of an audience of two hundred people for work purposes and did not experience debilitating anxiety or hours' worth of bathroom time before the event.

Melanie is not the only example of trauma resolution. Olivia, entered my program with debilitating anxiety that affected her life in many ways. Her anxiety primarily presented as dizziness and nausea, which she found frightening because it felt like she would lose control. It didn't make sense to her at the time, but her anxiety spiked whenever she felt slightly dizzy or nauseous because she feared she would do something she might regret. In fact, Olivia was terrified she might go crazy.

She was afraid to drive because she didn't trust herself to drive safely. She did not want to go on hikes with friends because she was scared she would take an accidental step off a cliff and fall to her death. She had stopped eating sugar or drinking caffeine because they made her feel shaky and nauseous and left her worried that she would lose control. She had restricted her diet to only eating foods she had prepared herself at home so that she knew, without doubt, there weren't any ingredients that might affect her. At a time when she should be hanging out with friends, socializing and exploring the world, Olivia was stuck, afraid to go anywhere or do anything, and she feared that anxiety would make her lose control of herself.

Olivia entered my program wanting to end anxiety and enjoy her twenties. The first step of the E.A.S.E. Method helped Olivia uncover an earlier experience in her adolescence that held the key to understanding her anxiety.

As many young people do, Olivia experimented with marijuana for the first time in her late adolescence. Unfortunately, her experience was marred with paranoia and irrational thoughts. Olivia smoked more than she had intended to and found herself imagining that her friends were saying nasty things about her. Scared and confused, so she left the party to go for a walk. She felt nauseous, dizzy, and desperately alone. The effects of marijuana left her feeling out of control. She was unable to discern what was real and what was imagined. Amid this discomfort, Olivia had a sudden, bizarre thought that she should jump in front of a car to make the feeling stop. She immediately felt afraid of the thought and terrified that, under the influence, she may go ahead and do so. When we spoke, she vehemently denied ever struggling with depression or experiencing a suicidal thought like this. This thought was out of character for her and scared her. As a result, she was sent into heightened states of fear and panic, desperately afraid that she was losing her mind. Eventually a friend found her on the street corner in the throes of a full-blown panic attack.

As you may imagine, that was the first and last experience Olivia had with substances. She was taken to the hospital that evening for a check-up and discharged with her diagnosis of anxiety and being stoned. But things changed dramatically after that day. Olivia continued to experience ongoing anxiety and a desperate fear that she would lose control of herself and do something she would regret.

Olivia thought the anxiety was a side effect of marijuana so she avoided any and all substances and ingredients that could alter her state of consciousness. She then went about desperately finding ways to manage her persistent anxiety. The more she tried to control the anxiety, the more the anxiety grew and the more afraid she became of the symptoms of nausea and dizziness. She restricted her diet and activities in increasing attempts to stay in control and reduce the anxiety. But the more she restricted herself, the stronger her self-doubt grew and the less she was able to trust herself.

The E.A.S.E. Method helped Olivia identify that the experience with marijuana was a traumatic event that needed processing. It was traumatizing to feel so out of control, dizzy, and nauseous and to believe that she could do something like jump in front of an oncoming car. The experience caused Olivia to believe that she could lose control at any second, especially if she didn't feel well. The intrusive thought she experienced, coupled with the panic attack that felt out of control, was evidence she used to keep believing that she could go crazy. So her anxiety began to alert her to keep her safe from herself. As the anxiety intensified, so did the symptoms of nausea and dizziness. Each time she felt dizzy or nauseous, her fear of losing control was triggered and created more anxiety. Olivia was experiencing anxiety about anxiety triggered by her traumatic experience in the past.

As she worked through the causes and reasons of anxiety, her fear began to make sense and she was able to begin challenging her self-doubt and mistrust. First, she learned to tolerate the symptoms in her body by reminding herself that they were just anxiety symptoms and not a re-living of the experience with marijuana. As she allowed herself more opportunities to be with anxiety, she gained confidence in her ability to stay in control despite uncomfortable feelings. Over time, she began to undo the fear that she could go crazy at any moment and started expanding her range of experience. By the time she finished the program, Olivia had been on a mountain hike with friends and returned to work. She was even willing to consider eating chocolate again.

These cases are not unique. Almost every single client I have worked with has identified a clear reason for the anxiety when they are prepared to lean in and listen. But it takes courage and the ability to accept the anxiety as a valid and purposeful response.

Anxiety always has something to tell you. When it has become stuck, it is simply screaming and afraid of itself, which means the anxiety is not functioning as it should. But then again, most things that have become stuck are not functioning as they should.

However, anxiety, in its ordinary state, is a response that really has your best interests and safety at heart. Yes, it has the potential to be quite disruptive, but at the heart of it, anxiety wants to help you. When you can lean in and listen, you might find areas that need attention, as Nora and Angela did. Other times, you might find a frightened amygdala that is stuck in a past little-T event like Melanie and Olivia did. Whatever you find, it simply requires your willingness to acknowledge and validate the cause or reason for anxiety, and then to address the need that is not being met. You really do have all it takes to shift anxiety back where it belongs: as an ordinary emotional response that comes and goes naturally.

Conclusion

I hope that the message is clear: Your emotional world, including anxiety, is a gift! Yes, feelings can be painful and they are not always easy to feel but they are there to guide us and they're what makes us so beautifully human. By fearing, dismissing or suppressing these emotions we only force them to get louder and, eventually, stuck.

It is time for us to move beyond misguided societal norms and expectations that invariably dull our rich emotional experiences. By pushing ourselves to be more 'normal' by feeling less we are creating a culture of disconnect between ourselves and our emotional guides. We lose sight of the loud messages that big, uncomfortable and disruptive feelings give us: That things are not as they should be and we need to pay attention.

This book has been focused on anxiety, but this applies to every emotion we have. Negative emotional responses serve an important purpose because they alert us to needs that are not being met. And the more we refuse to listen, the more we push them away and fear the experience, the more the emotion becomes stuck. If this goes on for long enough, we can become so overwhelmed that we cannot function as we would like to and we call ourselves crazy. You're not crazy. Your emotions are just stuck. And the solution is to slow down, pay attention, and listen.

Our greatest power lies in our ability to tolerate pain and grow from it. In fact, this is the place where true personal development occurs. As a baby takes their first steps, they fall and crash to the floor. Yes, it is painful, but they have learned a valuable lesson—don't step before the other foot has landed properly. Next time, they do things differently. Young children do not fear pain or making mistakes. They inherently know that this is how they grow. They cry their tears, they throw their tantrums, and they laugh with reckless abandon.

Then an adult enters the scene and asks the child to quiet down or pull it together. An adult draws attention to the mistakes they are making and attempts to correct them, putting emphasis on getting it right rather than the value of learning from our mistakes. And slowly, they begin to fear making mistakes because mistakes may cost them approval and threaten their sense of safety and need to belong.

Then, as that child enters primary school age, they come home with worries and disappointments. They cry about the mean things their friends have said and feel angry about the boundaries their parents have placed on them. And, as we know, the adults continue to tell them to "put their big kid panties on," "don't sweat the small stuff," and "let it go." Everyone works together to teach the child to push away those big feelings because no one feels comfortable being with them. Not the parents, and consequently, not the kids. This is how we all contribute to creating a culture that strives for "normalcy" and forgets that normal is actually emotional and messy.

The increasing number of teen suicides speaks volumes to the fact that our children are not being taught how to deal with emotions and the challenges of life. The stretched-thin mental health services and exceptionally long waitlists of people struggling with a range of mental health difficulties indicate that we have a very serious problem on our hands. People have become afraid of feeling. And in many cases, those emotions become stuck, stop functioning as they should, and become destructive. We label this "mental illness" and throw more drugs at the problem to stop all those pesky feelings from getting in the way of "being normal." By pretty much any metric you look at from children to adults, this approach to mental health is clearly not working.

Perhaps it is time to consider a different way of looking at our emotions and our humanity. Emotional responses need to be heard and validated. Let's accept and validate our emotions for ourselves and the people in our lives. Let's listen to what those feelings are saying. And let's use that wisdom to meet our needs, solve our problems, and make the world a better place.

People feel sad and lonely. That makes sense given what's been happening in our society. Despite the world becoming "more connected" with the advent of social media and the internet, people spend less time with their friends and family than ever before. They text instead of call, they scroll through social media instead of hanging out, they watch online videos instead of talking to one another. Maybe we're not meant to get our needs met through a screen. Maybe our sadness and loneliness are calling us to put our phones and computers down and spend more time with each other.

People feel angry. Their basic needs for shelter, health, and security are becoming harder to achieve, with house prices increasing and so many measurements of health and wellbeing declining. Their needs are not being met. And they are struggling to earn enough money to support and feed their families.

People feel anxious. We are constantly being told by journalists and social media that our world is dangerous and unsafe. Domestic violence, childhood sexual abuse, and neglect are prevalent. Politicians can't be trusted, quality and reliable healthcare is a scarcity, food prices are increasing, and recessions are forever looming. Our safety is not guaranteed, and in the current climate, our amygdalae are on high alert.

Pretending that everything is fine and trying to put a lid on all these emerging, messy feelings isn't helping us at all. We are not acknowledging our feelings or validating our experiences. The longer we ignore our emotions, the louder and more obvious our emotions will get until we pay attention. It's time to listen to our emotions, and to teach others to listen to theirs as well.

It can feel scary and difficult when you have never been shown how to do it, but that is the essence of the E.A.S.E. Method. These tools will help you understand your emotional experience of anxiety, accept it as real and valid, and find ways to meet the need it is calling you to pay attention to.

The steps in this book are designed to empower you with a different understanding of your anxiety and emotional world so we can remove the fear and stigma attached to stuck emotions. The steps of E.A.S.E. will help you form a better relationship with anxiety (and your other emotional responses), which helps your anxiety become unstuck. If you continue to use the principles of E.A.S.E. you will prevent anxiety from becoming stuck again in the future.

The E.A.S.E. Method is based on therapeutic techniques, and while clear steps are given here for implementing it in your own life, you might find it a little tricky to explore the deeper areas contributing to the anxiety. As a reader, you now have access to a dedicated reader portal with additional resources to help you do the work. If you need more help, I recommend you seek out a counselor or coach to assist you. There is no shame in needing support. And the strategies suggested in the E.A.S.E. Method can be easily applied to your own therapy, counseling, or coaching experience.

Now more than ever, it is important for us to learn how to be with our own emotional experiences, so that we can show those who come after us how to be with theirs. As we foster more tolerance for big, messy feelings, we show our own children how to tolerate theirs. And as we learn to listen to our emotional world and take guidance from it, we in turn show our youth how to listen to theirs. In this slow and steady way, we begin to show E.A.S.E. with our emotions and put an end to the stuck cycles of anxiety.

About the author

Diante Fuchs is a New Zealand-based Clinical Psychologist with over a decade of experience in private practice. Becoming frustrated with the exclusivity and limited reach of one-to-one, in-person therapy, Diante has trained as a certified anxiety coach and now offers online, group-based programs to individuals across the globe struggling with stuck anxiety.

While juggling her career, marriage, and parenting, Diante has experienced her own fair share of anxiety and has dedicated the past nine years to understanding the difference between ordinary anxiety and stuck anxiety. Through this process she has created the four-step E.A.S.E. Method, which she continues to use successfully with clients worldwide to help them shift anxiety.

Connect with Diante Fuchs

To find out more information visit her website:
www.theunstuckinitiative.com

Book Discounts and Special Deals

Sign up for free to get discounts and special deals
on our bestselling books at
www.TCKpublishing.com/bookdeals

Endnotes

1   World Health Organization (WHO) (2017) World Health Statistics 2017: Monitoring Health for the SDGs, Sustainable Development Goals. WHO, Geneva

2   COVID-19 Mental Disorders Collaborators (2021). Global prevalence and burden of depressive and anxiety disorders in 204 countries and territories in 2020 due to the COVID-19 pandemic. *Lancet (London, England)*, *398*(10312), 1700–1712.

3   GBD 2019 Mental Disorders Collaborators (2022). Global, regional, and national burden of 12 mental disorders in 204 countries and territories, 1990-2019: a systematic analysis for the Global Burden of Disease Study 2019. *The lancet. Psychiatry*, *9*(2), 137–150.

4   Sims, R., Michaleff, Z. A., Glasziou, P., & Thomas, R. (2021). Consequences of a Diagnostic Label: A Systematic Scoping Review and Thematic Framework. *Frontiers in public health*, *9*, 725877

5   Young, J. E., Klosko, J. S., & Weishaar, M. (2003). Schema therapy: A practitioner's guide. New York: Guilford.

6   American Psychiatric Association. (2013). *Diagnostic and statistical manual of mental disorders* (5th ed.).

7   Viner RM, Booy R, Johnson H, Edmunds WJ, Hudson L, Bedford H, Kaczmarski ED, et al. Outcomes of invasive meningococcal serogroup B disease in children and adolescents (MOSAIC): a case-control study. *Lancet Neurol.* 2012;**11**:774–783. doi: 10.1016/S1474-4422(12)70180-1.

8   Davies, M. R., Kalsi, G., Armour, C., Jones, I. R., McIntosh, A. M., Smith, D. J., Walters, J. T. R., Bradley, J. R., Kingston, N., Ashford, S., Beange, I., Brailean, A., Cleare, A. J., Coleman, J. R. I., Curtis, C. J., Curzons, S. C. B., Davis, K. A. S., Dowey, L. R. C., Gault, V. A., Goldsmith, K. A., … Breen, G. (2019). The Genetic Links to

Anxiety and Depression (GLAD) Study: Online recruitment into the largest recontactable study of depression and anxiety. *Behaviour research and therapy*, *123*, 103503.

9   Sullivan, D & Hardy B. P. (2021). The Gap and The Gain: The High Achievers' Guide to Happiness, Confidence, and Success. Hay House Publishing.

10   Sartori, S. B., Whittle, N., Hetzenauer, A., & Singewald, N. (2012). Magnesium deficiency induces anxiety and HPA axis dysregulation: modulation by therapeutic drug treatment. *Neuropharmacology*, *62*(1), 304–312.

11   Sahu, P., Thippeswamy, H., & Chaturvedi, S. K. (2022). Neuropsychiatric manifestations in vitamin B12 deficiency. *Vitamins and hormones*, *119*, 457–470.

12   Silva, M. R. M., Barros, W. M. A., Silva, M. L. D., Silva, J. M. L. D., Souza, A. P. D. S., Silva, A. B. J. D., Fernandes, M. S. S., Souza, S. L., & Souza, V. O. N. (2021). Relationship between vitamin D deficiency and psychophysiological variables: a systematic review of the literature. *Clinics (Sao Paulo, Brazil)*, *76*, e3155.

13   Bromberger JT, Kravitz HM, Chang Y, Randolph JF Jr, Avis NE, Gold EB, Matthews KA. Does risk for anxiety increase during the menopausal transition? Study of women's health across the nation. Menopause. 2013 May;20(5):488-95.

Printed in Great Britain
by Amazon

60059852R00111